Adobe®
Photoshop® CS3
Top 100
Tips & Tricks

Simplified®

TIPS & TRICKS

by Lynette Kent

Visual

BICENTENNIAL
1807
WILEY
2007
BICENTENNIAL

Wiley Publishing, Inc.

Adobe® Photoshop® CS3: Top 100 Simplified® Tips & Tricks

Published by
Wiley Publishing, Inc.
111 River Street
Hoboken, NJ 07030-5774

Published simultaneously in Canada

Copyright © 2007 by Wiley Publishing, Inc., Indianapolis, Indiana

Library of Congress Control Number: 2007931549

ISBN: 978-0-470-14476-3

Manufactured in the United States of America

10 9 8 7 6 5 4 3 2 1

Trademark Acknowledgments

Contact Us

For general information on our other products and services, contact our Customer Care Department within the U.S. at (800)762-2974, outside the U.S. at (317)572-3993, or fax (317)572-4002.

For technical support please visit www.wiley.com/techsupport.

Permissions

Wiley Publishing, Inc.

U.S. Sales

Contact Wiley at (800) 762-2974 or fax (317) 572-4002.

PRAISE FOR VISUAL BOOKS

"I have to praise you and your company on the fine products you turn out. I have twelve Visual books in my house. They were instrumental in helping me pass a difficult computer course. Thank you for creating books that are easy to follow. Keep turning out those quality books."
Gordon Justin (Brielle, NJ)

"What fantastic teaching books you have produced! Congratulations to you and your staff. You deserve the Nobel prize in Education. Thanks for helping me understand computers."
Bruno Tonon (Melbourne, Australia)

"A Picture Is Worth A Thousand Words! If your learning method is by observing or hands-on training, this is the book for you!"
Lorri Pegan-Durastante (Wickliffe, OH)

"Over time, I have bought a number of your 'Read Less - Learn More' books. For me, they are THE way to learn anything easily. I learn easiest using your method of teaching."
José A. Mazón (Cuba, NY)

"You've got a fan for life!! Thanks so much!!"
Kevin P. Quinn (Oakland, CA)

"I have several books from the Visual series and have always found them to be valuable resources."
Stephen P. Miller (Ballston Spa, NY)

"I have several of your Visual books and they are the best I have ever used."
Stanley Clark (Crawfordville, FL)

"Like a lot of other people, I understand things best when I see them visually. Your books really make learning easy and life more fun."
John T. Frey (Cadillac, MI)

"I have quite a few of your Visual books and have been very pleased with all of them. I love the way the lessons are presented!"
Mary Jane Newman (Yorba Linda, CA)

"Thank you, thank you, thank you...for making it so easy for me to break into this high-tech world."
Gay O'Donnell (Calgary, Alberta,Canada)

"I write to extend my thanks and appreciation for your books. They are clear, easy to follow, and straight to the point. Keep up the good work! I bought several of your books and they are just right! No regrets! I will always buy your books because they are the best."
Seward Kollie (Dakar, Senegal)

"I would like to take this time to thank you and your company for producing great and easy-to-learn products. I bought two of your books from a local bookstore, and it was the best investment I've ever made! Thank you for thinking of us ordinary people."
Jeff Eastman (West Des Moines, IA)

"Compliments to the chef!! Your books are extraordinary! Or, simply put, extra-ordinary, meaning way above the rest! THANKYOU THANKYOU THANKYOU! I buy them for friends, family, and colleagues."
Christine J. Manfrin (Castle Rock, CO)

CREDITS

Project Editor
Dana Rhodes Lesh

Sr. Acquisitions Editor
Jody Lefevere

Copy Editor
Dana Rhodes Lesh

Technical Editor
Dennis R. Cohen

Editorial Manager
Robyn Siesky

Business Manager
Amy Knies

Sr. Marketing Manager
Sandy Smith

Editorial Assistant
Laura Sinise

Manufacturing:
Allan Conley
Linda Cook
Paul Gilchrist
Jennifer Guynn

Book Design
Kathie Rickard

Production Coordinator
Adrienne L. Martinez

Layout
Jennifer Mayberry
Amanda Spagnuolo

Screen Artist
Jill A. Proll

Graphics
Ronda David-Burroughs
Cheryl Grubbs

Cover Design
Anthony Bunyan

Proofreader
Jennifer Stanley

Quality Control
Todd Lothery
Charles Spencer

Indexer
Broccoli Information Management

Wiley Bicentennial Logo
Richard J. Pacifico

Vice President and Executive Group Publisher
Richard Swadley

Vice President and Publisher
Barry Pruett

Composition Director
Debbie Stailey

ABOUT THE AUTHOR

Lynette Kent (Huntington Beach, CA) studied art and French at Stanford University. After completing her master's degree, she taught at both the high school and community college level. In addition to writing books and magazine articles, Lynette is adding to her portfolio, combining high-end photography and digital techniques. She often works at trade shows as a demo artist for computer graphics hardware and software companies. Her books on digital imaging and photography include *Photoshop CS2: Top 100 Simplified Tips & Tricks, Teach Yourself VISUALLY Digital Photography, Teach Yourself VISUALLY Mac OS X Leopard,* and *Scrapbooking with Photoshop Elements: The Creative Cropping Cookbook.* Lynette is also one of the leaders of the Adobe Technology Exchange of Southern California, a professional organization for graphic designers, photographers, and artists.

HOW TO USE THIS BOOK

Photoshop® CS3: Top 100 Simplified® Tips & Tricks includes 100 tasks that reveal cool secrets, teach timesaving tricks, and explain great tips guaranteed to make you more productive with Photoshop CS3. The easy-to-use layout lets you work through all the tasks from beginning to end or jump in at random.

Who is this book for?

You already know Photoshop basics. Now you would like to go beyond, with shortcuts, tricks, and tips that let you work smarter and faster. And because you learn more easily when someone *shows* you how, this is the book for you.

Conventions Used In This Book

① Steps

This book uses step-by-step instructions to guide you easily through each task. Numbered callouts on every screenshot show you exactly how to perform each task, step by step.

② Tips

Practical tips provide insights to save you time and trouble, caution you about hazards to avoid, and reveal how to do things with Photoshop CS3 that you never thought possible!

③ Task Numbers

Task numbers from 1 to 100 indicate which lesson you are working on.

④ Difficulty Levels

For quick reference, the symbol below the task number marks the difficulty level of each task.

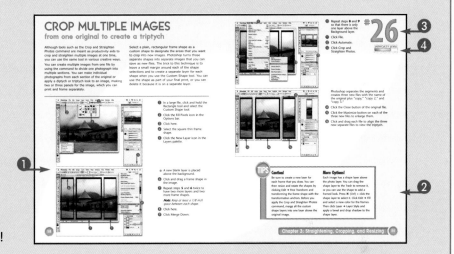

DIFFICULTY LEVEL — Demonstrates a new spin on a common task

DIFFICULTY LEVEL — Introduces a new skill or a new task

DIFFICULTY LEVEL — Combines multiple skills requiring in-depth knowledge

DIFFICULTY LEVEL — Requires extensive skill and may involve other technologies

Table of Contents

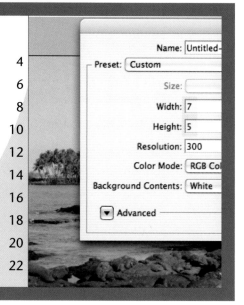

Photo © 2007 www.photospin.com

Table of Contents

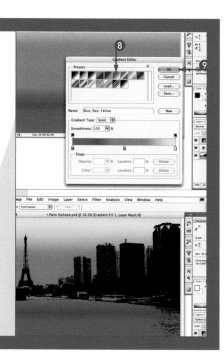

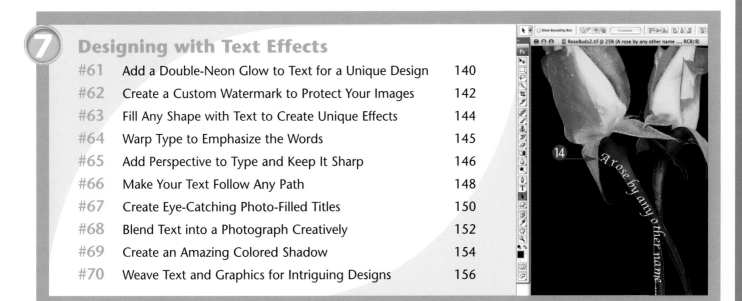

Table of Contents

Customizing Photoshop for Your Projects

Photoshop is an incredibly powerful program. Not only can you perform many different tasks with Photoshop, but you can also choose from a number of ways to accomplish each project. By setting Photoshop to work for you, you can develop your own techniques and find ways to adapt the standard tools to those techniques.

Learning to customize the application for your own personal projects and your own personal style makes your image editing more effective and efficient. When you work on an image, you may prefer to see some palettes and not others. You may also prefer certain tool settings to others. Setting up Photoshop to work your way makes you more productive, the program more useful, and everything you do with Photoshop much more fun.

With Photoshop CS3, Adobe has taken customization to a new level. You can now modify your settings and preferences in more ways than ever before by adjusting the workspace, the palettes, and the tools to fit the requirements of specific projects or just for your own preferences. These may seem like boring steps, yet setting up Photoshop's preferences and the workspace, knowing how to make your own gradients, customizing some shortcuts and tools, and designing templates and brushes can save you time as you work on images and free you to become more creative. By customizing Photoshop and setting the application your way, you gain familiarity with the program and become more comfortable as you try different projects.

Top 100

SELECT THE COLOR SETTINGS
for your projects

Using Adobe Photoshop CS3 is an image-altering experience! You can work on images for print or for the Web. You can improve photographs, repurpose them, or create original designs. Because printed images and Web images have different limits on the range of colors that they can represent, you need to set the working color space for your project.

Photoshop's default color space is set to sRGB, a very limited color space intended to be viewable on even the lowest-quality monitor. sRGB is a good color space for preparing Web images; however, it is a

much smaller color space than what better monitors can show and what printers can actually produce. Photographers and designers generally prefer the larger color space called Adobe RGB (1998), a good color space for working with photographs and projects that you plan to print.

In Photoshop CS3, you can easily choose your color space and save it as your own setting. Using the North America Prepress 2 settings and Adobe RGB (1998) will make your printed colors look much better.

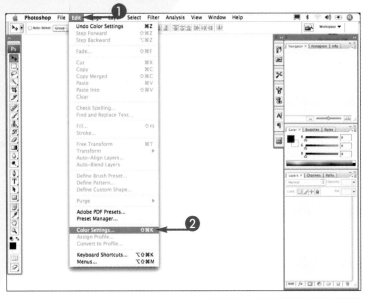

① Click Edit.

② Click Color Settings.

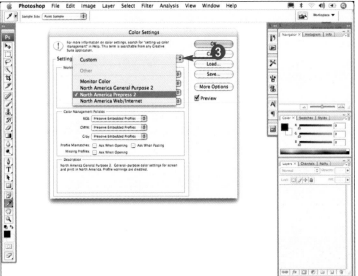

The Color Settings dialog box appears.

③ Click here and select North America Prepress 2.

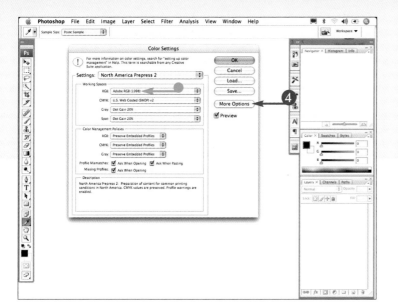

● The RGB setting changes to Adobe RGB (1998).

The rest of the Color Settings dialog box changes to reflect the preferred working space for images that you print.

④ Click More Options.

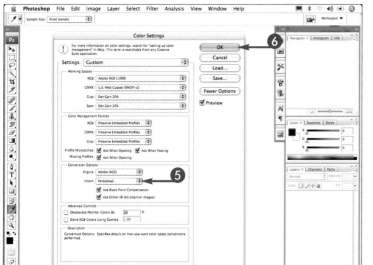

The dialog box expands.

⑤ Click here and select Perceptual for photography or Relative Colorimetric for a graphic design project.

⑥ Click OK.

Your color settings are saved until you reset your preferences.

TIPS

Customize It!

You can save your own Color Settings preset. The name of the preset changes to Custom when you deselect any check box or make any other changes. Click Save after customizing your settings. Type a name in the Save dialog box and click Save. Your customized preset appears in the Settings drop-down list, ready for you to choose.

Try This!

You can synchronize the color settings in other Creative Suite applications to match your saved custom Photoshop color settings. In Photoshop, click File and select Browse to launch the Bridge. Click Bridge and select Preferences (Mac) or Edit and select Preferences (PC). Click Advanced and click Enable Color Management In Bridge. Then from the Bridge, click Edit and select Creative Suite Color Settings. Click your saved custom color settings and click Apply.

SET THE PREFERENCES
for the way you work

In addition to Color Settings, Photoshop includes ten different panes in the Preferences dialog box. Although you can work with the default settings, changing some of these can make your computer run more efficiently, and changing others can make it easier to work with your projects. For example, by default, Photoshop is set to use more than half of the available RAM. You can lower this default setting depending on how much RAM you have installed in the computer and how many other applications you keep open at the same time. You can change the default colors for the guides

and grid when they are too similar to those in your image. Setting an additional plug-ins folder keeps third-party items separate from included Photoshop plug-ins, and setting a separate scratch disk can speed up your work on large files. Other personalized options, such as asking Photoshop to automatically launch the Bridge, can help you use Photoshop the way you want.

Read through each Preferences pane to familiarize yourself with the choices. Select the settings to fit your workflow and make Photoshop work for you.

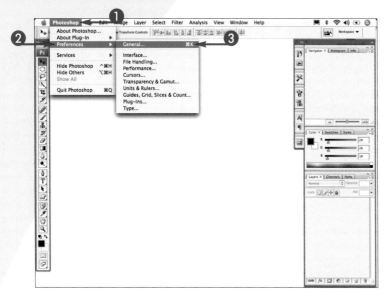

1 Click Photoshop (Edit).

2 Click Preferences.

3 Click General.

The General Preferences dialog box appears.

4 Click any arrows to change your settings.

5 Click to select the options you want or deselect those you do not want.

6 Click Next to continue customizing Preferences.

The dialog box changes to the Interface Preferences.

⑦ Click to select the options you want or deselect those you do not want.

⑧ Click Next.

⑨ Make any other changes that you prefer in the other Preferences panes.

⑩ Click OK when you have cycled through all the Preferences panes.

⑪ Click Photoshop (File).

⑫ Click Quit Photoshop (Exit).

The next time you start the application, your own settings take effect.

TIPS

Did You Know?
You can use keyboard shortcuts to set the Preferences. Press ⌘+K (Ctrl+K). Set your options for the General Preferences. Press ⌘+2 (Ctrl+2), and so on, for each of the ten Preferences panes.

Try This!
You can change the default Preferences so that just pressing the appropriate letter toggles each tool. In the General Preferences pane, deselect the Use Shift Key for Tool Switch check box.

Did You Know?
You can restore the Preferences any time by holding the ⌘+Option+ Shift (Ctrl+Alt+Shift) keys as you launch the application. Click Yes in the dialog box that appears, and the Preferences are reset to the defaults.

Customize your
PERSONAL WORKSPACE

The *workspace* in Photoshop refers to the layout of the different palettes and tools on your monitor screen. Photoshop CS3 enables you to design your own workspace so that you can easily access palettes or find the tools you need depending on the type of project. You can then save your custom workspace to reuse it with other images.

You can open the palettes that you use most and collapse others into buttons. You can move and resize individual palettes and docks. You can move the single-column toolbox, dock it, or change it to a

two-column toolbox. When you select the new Maximized Screen mode, your image automatically resizes as you adjust the tools and palettes. You can customize keyboard shortcuts and menus and save the current palette locations with your keyboard shortcuts and menu changes.

Photoshop CS3 also includes some preconfigured workspaces, and you can set up different workspaces to accommodate different tasks, such as one for color-correcting photographs and one for working with type.

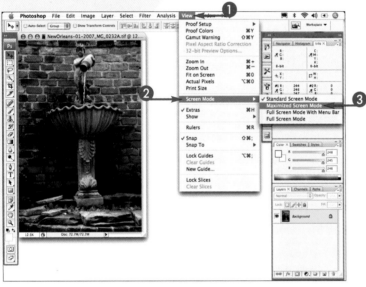

① With an image open, click View.

② Click Screen Mode.

③ Click Maximized Screen Mode.

The image onscreen changes to fill the space not occupied by other palettes.

④ Click here and drag the Layers palette group title bar to the left of the icon bar until a blue line appears.

⑤ Click here to reduce the Navigator and Color palette groups to icons with names.

● You can click here for any palette group to shrink it to a tabbed dock.

⑥ Click here and drag to the right to shrink the Navigator and Color docks to icons only.

The image window automatically adjusts to fit the space with each change.

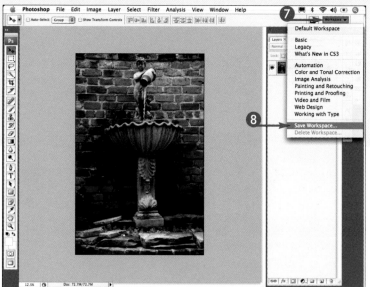

Note: *You can make any changes you prefer for your custom workspace.*

⑦ Click Workspace.

⑧ Click Save Workspace.

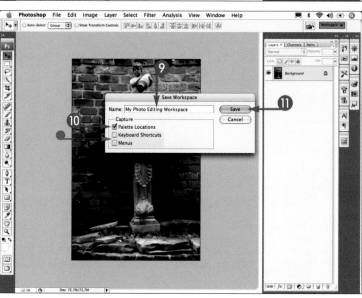

The Save Workspace dialog box appears.

⑨ Type a name for your workspace.

⑩ Make sure that the Palette Locations check box is selected.

● You can select Keyboard Shortcuts and Menus to save any other changes you make.

⑪ Click Save.

Your custom workspace is saved.

TIPS

Did You Know?

You can return to the original workspace any time by clicking Window → Workspace → Default Workspace. You can also delete unused workspaces by clicking Window → Workspace → Delete Workspace and selecting the one that you want to delete.

More Options!

Photoshop CS3 includes a number of predesigned workspaces for particular projects, such as Color and Tonal Correction and Painting and Retouching. Click Window → Workspace and select a workspace from the lower section of the submenu.

More Options!

You can color-code the menu items that you use most often. Click Edit → Menus. In the dialog box that appears, click the expand triangle next to a menu name. Click None and select a color from the submenu.

PERSONALIZE YOUR VIEW
of the Bridge

The Bridge that ships with Photoshop CS3 acts as a power browser and central hub for all the Creative Suite 3 applications and shows all types of files and folders that are available. You can even see thumbnails of documents and files from other applications, such as Word or Acrobat files. When you double-click a thumbnail from the Bridge, the other application launches. You can open the Bridge from within Photoshop or as a separate application.

The Bridge offers different ways to search, categorize, and view your files, options for adding

information, and automation for various repetitive tasks.

By customizing and saving your own Bridge workspace, you can review and compare images more efficiently and have more fun doing so.

To launch the Bridge from within Photoshop, click File → Browse, click the Go to Bridge icon in the Options bar, or press the keyboard shortcut ⌘+opt+O (Ctrl+Alt+O).

① Launch the Bridge.

Note: You can make any changes you prefer for your custom workspace.

② Click the Folders tab to navigate to a folder of images.

③ Click and drag the Metadata and Keywords tabs to the left panel between the Folders and the Filter tab.

④ Click and drag the Preview tab to the center pane.

⑤ Click and drag the Content tab to the right pane.

The Content images align vertically on the right.

⑥ Click an image to see it in the Preview tab.

⑦ Click here and drag to the right.

The Preview tab enlarges.

● You can also click the separator bar on the left to enlarge the Preview tab more.

⑧ Click and hold the first workspace button.

A menu appears.

⑨ Click Save Workspace.

The Save Workspace dialog box appears.

⑩ Type a name for the workspace.

⑪ Make sure that both check boxes are checked.

● Optionally, you can click here and select any key not already assigned by the Bridge to a keyboard shortcut.

⑫ Click Save.

Your custom workspace is saved as the default for the first button.

Note: You can change the default settings for the other two workspace buttons by following the preceding steps with different settings.

More Options!
You can sort by different parameters using the Filter panel. For example, you can view only the portrait-orientation images or all the images created on a specific date.

More Options!
Press Option (Alt) and click multiple images in the Content palette to compare them in the Preview panel. You can also stack the group to keep them together by clicking Stacks → Group as Stack or pressing ⌘+G.

Enlarge It!
You can expand your preview to fill your screen by pressing Tab. The Preview window fills the screen and the other palettes slide away on the sides. Press Tab again to return to your custom Bridge workspace.

ADD YOUR OWN KEYBOARD SHORTCUT
for a favorite filter

Photoshop includes keyboard shortcuts for a variety of tasks. You can work more efficiently if you use shortcuts for the tools that you use most often. Many of the tools in the toolbox already have keyboard shortcuts assigned. Still, you may find yourself going to the menu to select an item, such as the Gaussian Blur filter, so often that a personalized keyboard shortcut is very useful and a huge timesaver.

You can easily create your own custom keyboard shortcuts to fit your workflow. You can even change the ones that Photoshop has already assigned to

something that you can remember better. If the keyboard shortcut that you choose is already assigned by Photoshop for another function, a warning appears. You should also avoid keyboard shortcuts that are used by your operating system. You can change Photoshop's default shortcuts, or you can try a different set of keystrokes that are not already assigned.

Learning and using custom keyboard shortcuts can streamline your workflow, leaving you more time for designing and photo editing.

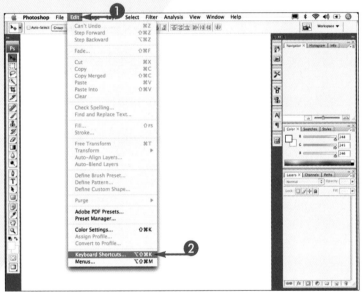

① Click Edit.

② Click Keyboard Shortcuts.

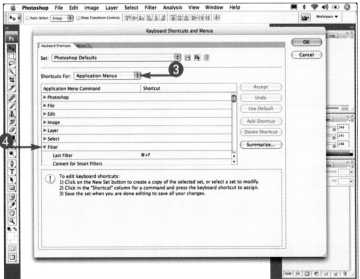

The Keyboard Shortcuts and Menus dialog box appears.

③ Click here and select Application Menus.

④ Click the Filter expand arrow.

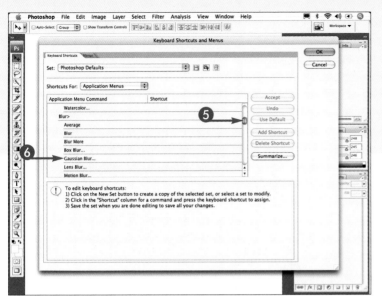

The filters are listed along with any existing keyboard shortcuts.

⑤ Scroll down to the filter to which you want to add a shortcut.

⑥ Click the filter.

# 5

DIFFICULTY LEVEL

The filter is highlighted, and an empty data field appears under the Shortcut column.

⑦ Press ⌘ (Ctrl) and type your shortcut in the data field.

Note: A shortcut must contain either ⌘ (Ctrl) or an F key in the name.

⑧ Click Accept.

The Photoshop Defaults set is modified to include your shortcut.

⑨ Click OK to finish adding your custom keyboard shortcut.

TIPS

Did You Know?

The Keyboard Shortcuts and Menus dialog box is found under both the Edit menu and the Window → Workspace menu. You can also access the Keyboard Shortcuts and Menus dialog box by using a keyboard shortcut — ⌘+Shift+ Option+K (Ctrl+Shift+Alt+K).

Try This!

You can save a list of the default Photoshop keyboard shortcuts or your customized shortcuts. Click Summarize in the Keyboard Shortcuts and Menus dialog box and save the file as Photoshop Defaults.htm. Open the file and print the list for reference.

More Options!

Click the Shortcuts For arrow to select Palette Menus or Tools. Then click the expand arrow next to the palette name or tool and type your shortcut. You can even save a keyboard shortcut set with a custom workspace!

CREATE A CUSTOM ACTION
to increase your efficiency

Performing repeated steps is boring and time-consuming. That is why Adobe created actions and the Actions palette. An *action* is a series of commands that you can apply to an image with one click of the mouse. Unlike a keyboard shortcut, which can only invoke a command, an action can open a command, apply changes to an image, step through another command, apply it, and even save a file in a particular way. You can create your own actions for steps that you do over and over, save the actions, and add them to the Actions palette.

To create an action, you first record a sequence of steps. You then name and save your new action in the Actions palette. The next time that you need to apply the same steps to an image, you play the action, and Photoshop automatically applies the series of operations to the open file or even to an entire folder of files.

Actions are easy to create, and they can help you automate your work for repetitive tasks, leaving you more time to work on creative projects.

❶ Open an image.

❷ Click the Actions button to open the Actions palette.

❸ Click the Create New Action button.

● Alternatively, you can click here and select New Action.

The New Action dialog box appears.

❹ Type the name of your action.

❺ Click here and select a keyboard shortcut.

❻ Click here and select a color for the action.

❼ Click Record.

● The Record button in the Actions palette turns red.

❽ Perform the steps on the image that you want to record as an action.

Note: As an example, the following steps show creating an action of opening a new 7" x 5" document at 300 pixels/inch for a greeting card.

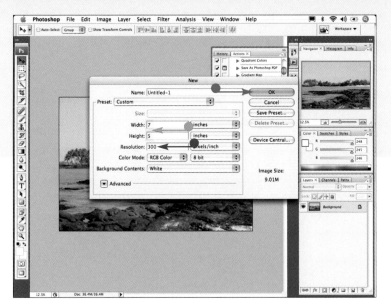

Press ⌘+N (Ctrl+N) to open a new file.

The New file dialog box appears.

● Type your specific dimensions in the Width and Height fields.

● Type **300**, or your desired resolution, in the Resolution field.

● Click OK.

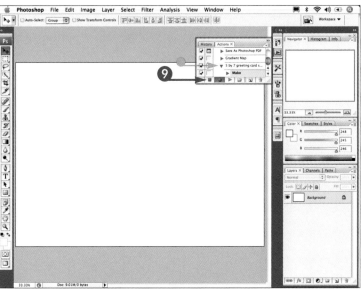

A new untitled document appears.

❾ After you perform the last step of your action, click the Stop Recording button.

● Your custom action is now recorded and is listed in the Actions palette.

You can test your action by clicking the keyboard shortcut that you assigned.

TIPS

More Options!

You can apply an action to a folder of files by clicking File → Automate → Batch and selecting the action and a source folder. Or you can apply an action to a group of images from the Bridge by clicking Tools → Photoshop → Batch.

Try This!

You can make the actions easier to find by selecting Button Mode in the Actions palette's drop-down menu. Your actions change to color-coded buttons.

Did You Know?

You can load other prerecorded actions such as Frames or Image Effects included with Photoshop CS3 by clicking the Actions palette's drop-down menu and clicking a set in the bottom section of the menu.

DESIGN A CUSTOMIZED BRUSH
with your settings

Whether you retouch photographs, design brochures, or paint from scratch, you will use the Brush tools many times and in many ways. Selecting the Brush tool from the toolbox opens a variety of brushes in the drop-down menu on the Options bar.

You can modify the size, roundness, or other attributes of any of the existing brushes to suit your drawing style or your image. You can then save the modified brush as your own custom brush so that it is ready to use for your next design.

A number of other tools also have modifiable brush options, including the Pencil tool, the Eraser tool, the Clone Stamp tool, the Pattern Stamp tool, the History Brush, the Art History Brush, the Blur tool, the Sharpen tool, the Smudge tool, the Dodge tool, the Burn tool, and the Sponge tool.

Customizing Brush tools for your projects is a timesaving technique, and it is fun. You may find yourself experimenting with all types of brushes.

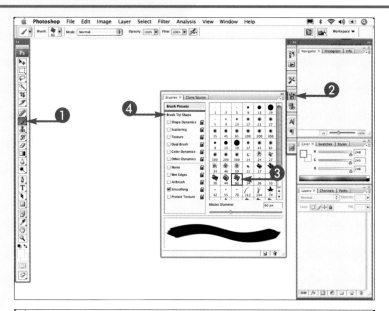

1 Click the Brush tool.

2 Click the Brushes button to open the Brushes palette.

3 Click the preset brush that you want to modify into a custom brush.

4 Click Brush Tip Shape.

The shape choices are now visible.

5 Click and drag any of the sliders to change the size and look.

6 Drag the black handles and gray arrow to alter the roundness and brush angle.

● Watch the Preview window to see the brushstroke change.

7 Click another attribute that you want to change, such as Dual Brush.

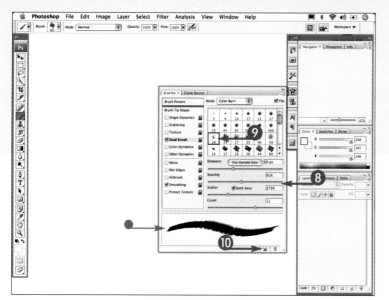

The window changes to display new settings.

⑧ Click and drag any of the sliders to change the size and look.

⑨ Click another selection in the window.

● Watch the Preview window to see the brushstroke change more.

⑩ Click the New Brush button at the bottom of the palette.

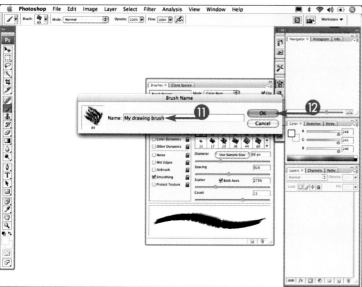

The Brush Name dialog box appears.

⑪ Type a name for your brush.

⑫ Click OK.

Your customized brush is stored with the Photoshop CS3 Preferences.

TIPS

Caution!

Save your custom brushes to avoid losing them if you reset Photoshop's Preferences. Click the drop-down menu on the Brushes palette and select Save Brushes. Name the file with the suffix .abr and click Save.

Did You Know?

Photoshop CS3 includes many different brush files listed at the bottom of the submenus on the Brushes palette or Brush options menu in the Options bar. You can load any set by clicking its name.

More Options!

You can view the brushes listed by name rather than the stroke thumbnail. Click the drop-down menu on the Brushes palette and click Text Only or select a different-sized thumbnail or list view.

MAKE A SPECIAL GRADIENT
to suit your design

The Gradient tool helps you blend multiple colors as you fill an area in an image. You can use the Gradient tool in many ways, such as by itself to fill text with soft gradations of color, to fill backgrounds with a gradient, or in combination with layers and masks. Gradients are often used when making composite images. Photoshop includes default gradient color sets and has other gradient sets listed in the drop-down menu in the Options bar. You can also create your own gradient by sampling colors from areas in your image or choosing different colors altogether.

You can add intermediate colors and design a blend among multiple colors in any order that you want. You can even design gradients that fade from any color to transparent.

You can also choose a style for the gradient, such as linear, radial, angled, reflected, or diamond. You customize the gradients from the Gradient Editor. Start with an existing gradient and modify the colors, the color stops, and other variations in the dialog box. The possibilities are almost endless!

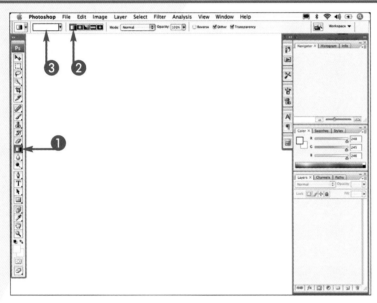

① Click the Gradient tool.

② Click a gradient type in the Options bar.

③ Click inside the gradient thumbnail in the Options bar.

The Gradient Editor dialog box appears.

④ Click the left color stop under the gradient bar to select it.

⑤ Click the Color thumbnail to choose a new color.

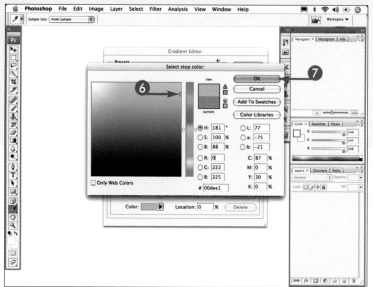

The Color Picker dialog box appears.

⑥ Select a color from the dialog box.

Note: If you have an image open, you can move the cursor over the image to select a color.

⑦ Click OK.

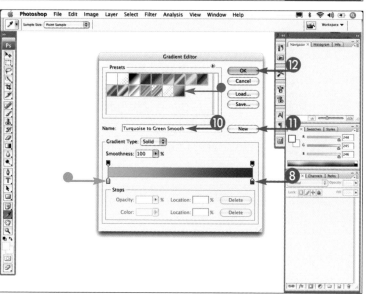

● The selected color fills the left color stop in the Gradient Editor.

⑧ Click the right color stop under the gradient bar to select it.

⑨ Repeat steps **5** to **7** to select the colors for the right color stop.

⑩ Type a name for your new gradient in the Name field.

⑪ Click New.

● The custom gradient appears in the presets.

⑫ Click OK.

TIPS

Caution!

You must save your custom gradients in a presets library to avoid losing them when you reset Photoshop's Preferences. Click Save in the Gradient Editor dialog box or choose Save Gradients from the drop-down menu in the Gradient Picker. Type a name for your gradient library with the suffix .grd. Click Save, and your gradients are saved in Photoshop's presets.

More Options!

You can duplicate any of the color stops to vary your custom gradient. Press Option (Alt) and drag the first color stop to another location. Pressing Option (Alt), you can even drag a new color stop over other color stops and drop it in a different position. To remove a color stop, click the stop and drag straight down.

CALIBRATE AND PROFILE
your monitor for better editing

You adjust colors in Photoshop based on what you see on the screen. Because each monitor displays color differently and because those characteristics change over time, you should calibrate and profile your monitor regularly to make sure that you are viewing the colors that are actually in your files.

Calibration is the process of setting your monitor to an established color standard. *Profiling* is the process of creating an International Color Consortium (ICC) profile, a description of how your monitor reproduces color.

Although the Macintosh System Preferences includes a display-calibration tool and Photoshop CS3 installs the Adobe Gamma utility on Windows, these software-only methods are very subjective. Using a hardware-calibration device is an easier and more accurate method of adjusting your monitor. Both X-Rite and ColorVision make affordable devices. A *colorimeter* corrects the color on your screen. A *spectrophotometer* measures and adjusts color for both your monitor and printer.

You can easily make your monitor display accurate color using the X-Rite i1 Display LT colorimeter or the X-Rite i1 Photo LT spectrophotometer.

Note: The following steps are those used for either the X-Rite i1 Display LT or the X-Rite i1 Photo LT.

① Install the X-Rite i1 Match software included with the device, launch it, and plug the device into a USB port.

Note: Macintosh users should be logged in as the Admin account.

② Click the monitor image.

③ Click Easy.

④ Click the Forward button.

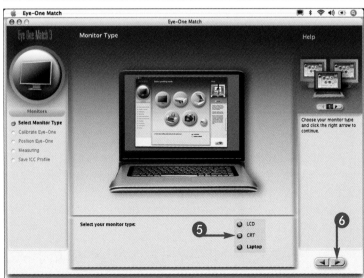

The Monitor Type screen appears.

⑤ Click to select your monitor type.

⑥ Click the Forward button.

⑦ Place your i1 Display on a black surface or place the i1 Pro in its cradle and click Calibrate.

⑧ Click the Forward button to continue.

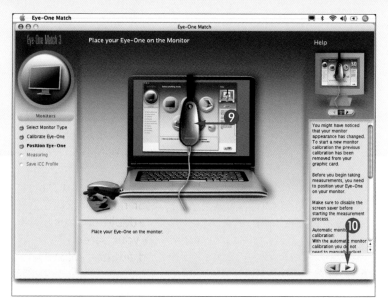

The Place Your Eye-One screen appears.

9 Place the unit on the monitor as the image shows.

10 Click the Forward button.

The screen goes black, and then a box appears under the colorimeter on the screen.

The box fills with white, then black, and then colors as the device automatically measures the color presentation capabilities of your monitor.

● A new screen appears, showing the name of the monitor profile created by the device.

11 Click here to select a reminder for the next calibration.

12 Click the Forward button.

A dialog box appears, telling you where the profile was saved on your computer's hard drive.

13 Click OK.

14 Quit the i1 Match software application and disconnect the i1 Colorimeter or Spectrophotometer.

9

DIFFICULTY LEVEL

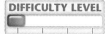

TIPS

Did You Know?

As monitors age, they lose their color accuracy more quickly. Calibrate and profile regularly — monthly if your monitor is new or weekly if your monitor is over two years old.

Important!

Clean the monitor screen with a soft cloth before you start, but never spray any cleaning liquids on your monitor. CRT monitors need to warm up for 30 minutes before you calibrate and create a profile.

More Options!

X-Rite's i1 Match software keeps a Help file open in a column along the right side of the screen. You can increase your understanding of color calibration by reading an explanation of each step as you proceed.

Turn on the full power of Photoshop with a
PEN TABLET

Using a mouse as an input device may work for placing insertion points in text or dragging a rectangular selection in Photoshop, but using a Brush tool or selecting specific areas with a mouse is similar to writing your name with a bar of soap — clunky and inaccurate. Using a pressure-sensitive tablet and pen, such as the Wacom Intuos, instead of a mouse enables you to edit images with greater comfort and control. Instead of scooting the mouse around, you place the cursor exactly where you want to be with the pen, so you become more productive.

Using a tablet and pen, you have access to many Photoshop tools that are only available when a tablet is connected to the computer. You can easily make precise selections, create blended composite images, and even paint digitally as you would with a traditional paintbrush on paper.

The key to using a tablet and pen and turning on the full power of Photoshop is to start by setting the Tablet Preferences located in the System Preferences or Control Panel.

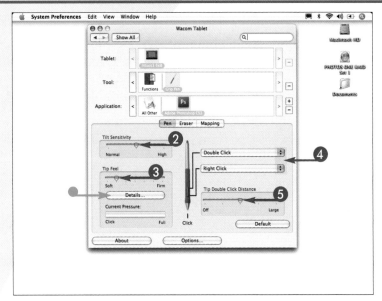

① Open the Tablet Preferences.

② Click and drag the Tilt Sensitivity slider to the right for greater tilt response.

③ Drag the Tip Feel slider for a softer or firmer touch.

● You can click Details to test your settings.

④ Click the arrows and select a different keystroke for the rocker switch.

⑤ Drag the Tip Double Click Distance slider to reduce or increase the sensitivity.

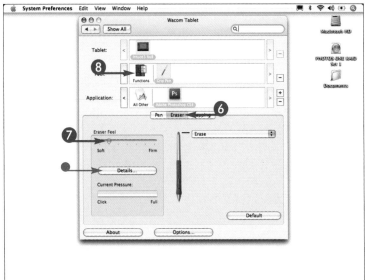

⑥ Click the Eraser tab.

The Eraser Preferences appear.

⑦ Click and drag the Eraser Feel slider for softer or firmer eraser pressure.

● You can click Details to test your settings.

⑧ Click the Functions tool to customize the tablet keys.

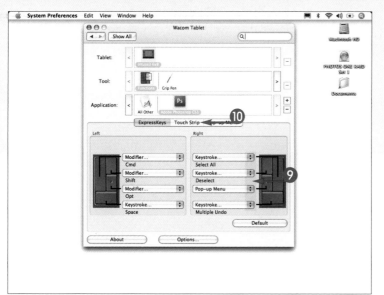

The ExpressKeys Preferences appear.

⑨ Click the arrows to change the settings for the tablet keys.

⑩ Click the Touch Strip tab.

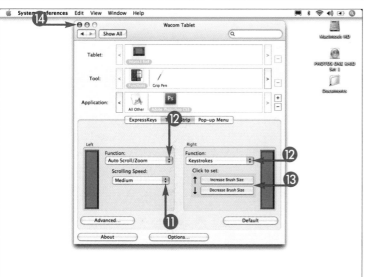

The Touch Strip Preferences appear.

⑪ Click here to change the scrolling speed.

⑫ Click the Function arrows and select different functions.

⑬ Click in the Click to Set boxes.

In the dialog box that appears, type your keystroke preferences in the Keys data field and click OK.

⑭ Click the Close button.

Your custom settings are saved in the Preferences.

Try This!
You can select specific settings for each individual application. Click the + to the right of the Application section and select Photoshop CS3 or another application. Set the options for the keys you use most in Photoshop.

Did You Know?
The Wacom Intuos is considered the most responsive pen tablet on the market. The Wacom pen feels like any pen or pencil, and the ExpressKeys and Touch Strip can help you become more productive.

Did You Know?
Over 20 Photoshop tools are specifically designed for use with a pressure-sensitive tablet and pen. Without a tablet attached to your computer, a warning sign appears for many of the settings in the Brushes palette.

Working with Layers, Selections, and Masks

Unless you use Photoshop only to resize and print photographs, you will use layers, selections, and masks in some way for most projects. You may duplicate a layer as a safety step or build a complex multilayered image file with any combination of layers, selections, and masks.

Layers give real editing and designing power to Photoshop. A *layer* is basically a transparency sheet with an image on it. You can edit, transform, or add filters to a layer independently from other layers. You can make one layer alter the look of a layer above or below it. You can save a file with the layers and easily change your design later by editing one or more of the layers. You can also drag a layer from one document to another to copy it.

Selections enable you to isolate areas in your image and apply different effects or filters without affecting the rest of the image. You can even select areas on one layer and create a new layer with that selection. You can make selections with many Photoshop tools depending on the type of area that you need to isolate. You can copy, move, paste, and save selections.

You can use masks to block out one area of an image or protect it from manipulations. A *mask* is a selection shown as a grayscale image: The white areas are selected; the black areas are not. You can create bitmap layer masks with painting tools or resolution-independent vector masks with a shape tool.

Top 100

DUPLICATE AND CHANGE THE BACKGROUND LAYER

to fix problems such as overexposure

The Background layer is the bottommost image in the Layers palette — and the only layer when you first open a new photograph. You can duplicate the Background layer and change the blending mode to change the look or simply work on the duplicated layer without altering the original.

Although it does increase the file size, working on a duplicated layer works well for simple changes and can be used as a safety step in various workflows. With a duplicate Background layer, you can quickly compare your modified image with the original by clicking the Visibility icon, the leftmost box next to the layer thumbnail in the Layers palette, to hide the duplicated layer and view only the original Background layer. Then you can click the Visibility icon on again to see the changes you made.

Photoshop CS3 includes many different types of layers. You can add layers above the Background layer for various effects. You can convert this layer and move it in the Layers palette. Layers are the key to nondestructive image editing — working on your images without damaging existing pixels.

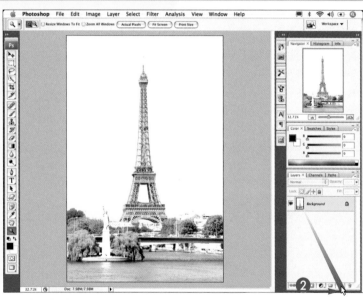

Note: This task is shown in the Maximized screen mode.

1 Open an overexposed image in Photoshop.

2 In the Layers palette, click and drag the Background layer thumbnail over the New Layer button and release the mouse button.

Photoshop places a duplicated Background layer above the original.

3 Double-click the Background copy's name in the Layers palette to highlight it.

4 Type a different name for the copy.

5 Click here and change the blend mode to Multiply.

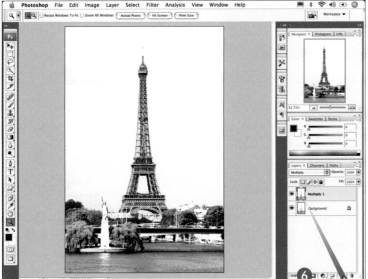

The photo appears darker.

*Note: If the photo is still overexposed, follow steps **6** and **7**. If it appears too dark, go directly to step **8**.*

6 Click and drag the copy layer over the New Layer button and release the mouse button.

7 Repeat step **6** until the photo appears slightly dark.

#11

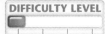
DIFFICULTY LEVEL

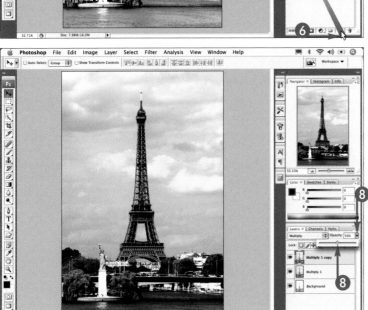

8 Click here and drag the slider to the left to lower the opacity of the top layer until the photo appears properly exposed.

Note: There are many other uses for duplicating the Background layer, such as to protect the original image when you apply certain filters or retouching portraits.

TIPS

Did You Know?
You can duplicate the Background layer or any other layer with a keyboard shortcut. Click the layer to be duplicated in the Layers palette to select it. Press ⌘+J (Ctrl+J). The layer is quickly duplicated.

Did You Know?
The selected layer is called the *active layer.* You can select multiple layers by pressing ⌘ (Ctrl) and clicking them, and then you can move them together or apply styles to them all at the same time.

More Options!
To move the Background layer, you must unlock it by double-clicking its name, typing a new name in the dialog box that appears, and clicking OK. You can then move that layer in the Layers palette for more editing options.

Using an
ADJUSTMENT LAYER
to adjust a photo nondestructively

You can make a variety of adjustments to an image by using the Adjustments option on the Image menu. If you made a duplicate of your Background layer, you can adjust your photo using the duplicate and not alter the original layer. However, each time you change the pixels in an image, you lose some data. If you combine adjustments, you lose even more pixel information.

By applying an adjustment layer instead, you can apply color and tonal changes to your image without changing any pixel values.

With an adjustment layer, you can try various settings and edit the adjustment at a later time. You can reduce or vary the effect of the adjustment by using the Opacity or Fill sliders. You can also combine various adjustment layers. An adjustment layer affects all the layers below it.

Photoshop includes a number of different types of adjustment layers, which you access through the Layer menu.

Note: This task is shown in the Maximized screen mode.

① Click Layer.

② Click New Adjustment Layer.

③ Click to select the adjustment that you want to make — for example, Levels.

The New Layer dialog box appears.

④ Type a name for the adjustment layer.

⑤ Click OK.

The dialog box for the type of adjustment layer you selected appears.

Note: Make sure that the Preview box is checked.

⑥ For Levels, drag this slider to the right until it is just below the rise of the black histogram on the left side.

⑦ For Levels, drag this slider to the left until it is just below the rise of the black histogram on the right side.

⑧ For Levels, drag this slider slightly to adjust the midtones if necessary.

Note: Different adjustment layers' dialog boxes have different options. Make the changes your adjustment layer type requires.

⑨ Click OK.

The adjustment layer's changes are applied to the image.

⑩ Repeat steps **1** and **2**.

⑪ Select a different adjustment layer, such as Exposure.

The dialog box for the type of adjustment layer you selected appears.

⑫ For Exposure, click here and drag slightly to the left or right to adjust the exposure.

Note: Make the needed changes to the options that are available for your adjustment layer type.

⑬ Click OK.

The adjustment layer's changes are applied to the image.

⑭ Click here to turn off the Visibility icon for each adjustment layer and hide the adjustment.

⑮ Compare the effect of the adjustment layers.

Note: If you do not like the effect of an adjustment layer, you can simply delete that layer.

12

TIPS

Did You Know?

You can use an empty adjustment layer and change the Layer blending mode to get the same effect as duplicating a layer and changing the blending mode. Simply click Layer → New Adjustment Layer and select any one of the adjustments. Do not make any changes in the dialog box and click OK. Change the blending mode of the empty adjustment layer as you would with any duplicated layer.

More Options!

All adjustment layers include a layer mask, represented by a white icon next to the adjustment layer icon in the Layers palette. You can click the layer mask and paint with black to limit where the adjustment affects the underlying image. If you accidentally reveal too much of the underlying image, you can change the foreground color to white and paint in the mask to reapply more of the adjustment.

BLEND TWO PHOTOS TOGETHER
with a layer mask

Layer masks open a world of imaging possibilities that you just cannot create with traditional tools. Using a layer mask to hide parts of one image and reveal parts of another, you can design images that are sure to grab a viewer's attention.

You can create very dramatic effects using a layer mask to blend one photograph into another. For example, you can blend a photograph of a wedding couple into a photo of the bride's bouquet. You can also create comical effects with this technique if, for example, you blend a photo of a potato with a photo of a person lying on a couch.

You can start by blending with a gradient on the mask and touch it up with a brush or simply brush on the mask. As you paint with black on a white layer mask, the top image becomes visible. If you paint away too much, simply reverse the colors and paint with white.

This technique is especially effective using a pen tablet. By setting the painting brush to respond to pen pressure, you can easily control how much of the image you reveal with each brush stroke.

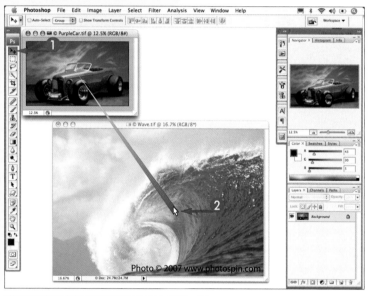

① With the two photographs you want to blend open, click the Move tool.

② Click and drag the photo you want to blend on top of the photo you want for the base.

Optionally, you can click and drag the top image layer to adjust the position on the base image if necessary.

Note: If the images are the same size and resolution, the top image will hide the base image.

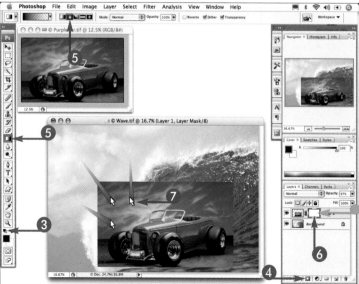

③ Click here to set the default colors so that the Foreground color is black.

④ Click the Layer Mask button.

● A white layer mask appears in the Layers palette.

⑤ Click the Gradient tool and select a gradient style from the Options bar.

⑥ Click the layer mask to select it.

⑦ Click and drag in the image to apply the gradient to the mask.

Note: You may need to click and drag several times to get the effect that you want.

The two images blend together.

8️⃣ Click the Brush tool.

9️⃣ Select a large soft-edge brush from the Brush drop-down palette.

🔟 Paint in the image using black to touch up the mask and reveal more of the background photo.

DIFFICULTY LEVEL

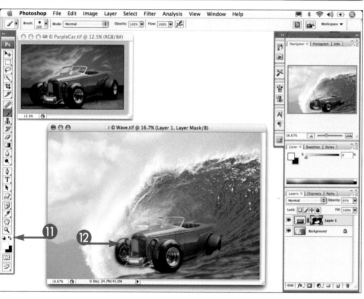

1️⃣1️⃣ Click here to reverse the foreground and background colors.

1️⃣2️⃣ Paint with white to fill in areas where you have painted away too much of the base image.

The white paint strokes bring some edge details of the base image back, making the top image appear to blend into the base image.

TIPS

Try This!
Using a Wacom pen tablet, you can vary your paint strokes with pen pressure. Click the Brushes icon to open the Brushes Presets. Click Shape Dynamics and set Size Jitter Control to Pen Pressure.

More Options!
Type some text with the Type tool and click the Layer Mask button in the Layers palette. Paint over some areas of the letters with black to hide them to make the text appear from behind parts of the image.

Customize It!
Double-click the Foreground Color button in the toolbox and select a gray in the Color Picker. Paint some areas of the layer mask with gray to make them only partially visible.

Using
CUSTOM SHAPE LAYERS
to add designs to photos

Photoshop CS3 includes a variety of predesigned custom shapes you can apply using the Custom Shape tool. You can also create your own shape with the Pen tools. Custom shapes are resolution-independent vector shapes, meaning that they maintain crisp edges when resized or saved in a PDF file. You can add shapes to any image as a design element or to alter the shape of a photo.

You can access more custom shapes than the default set by clicking the Custom Shape icon in the Options bar and clicking the shape icon drop-down arrow to open the selection menu. When you click the drop-down arrow on that menu, you can select one of the shape groups at the bottom of the menu or select All to see all the installed shapes at once. Then double-click a shape thumbnail to select it.

When using shapes, you will see two boxes in the Layers palette: the fill layer and a linked vector mask. The mask is the shape's outline. You can choose the fill layer's color in the Options bar before you draw the shape or set the fill color to a zero opacity fill.

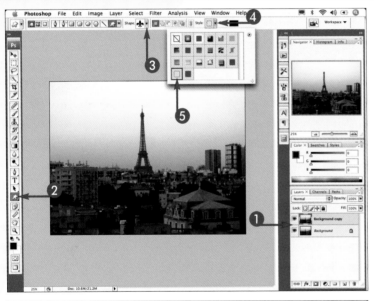

Note: This task is shown in the Maximized screen mode.

① Duplicate the Background layer of an image.

Note: To create a duplicate of your Background layer, see Task #11.

② Click the Custom Shape tool.

③ Click here, double-click a shape, and close the selection box.

④ Click here.

⑤ Double-click the 0 percent opacity icon.

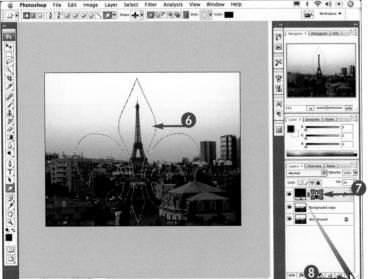

⑥ Click and drag in your image to draw the shape.

⑦ Press ⌘+click (Ctrl+click) the layer thumbnail.

The shape changes to a selection.

⑧ Click the shape layer thumbnail in the Layers palette and drag it to the layer Trash.

The selection remains on the image.

⑨ Press D to reset the foreground and background colors to the default.

⑩ Press X to reverse the default colors, making white the foreground color.

⑪ Press ⌘+J (Ctrl+J) to duplicate the selection onto its own layer.

● The selection is on the new layer and not visible on the image.

⑫ Click the Background copy layer to select it.

⑬ Click Layer → New Fill Layer → Gradient.

⑭ Click OK when the New Layer dialog box appears.

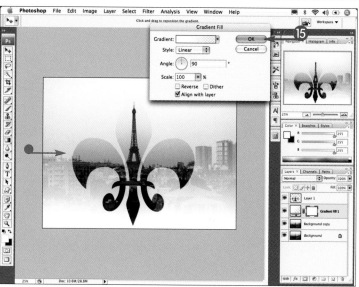

● The base image is covered with a white-to-transparent gradient fill.

⑮ Click OK in the Gradient Fill dialog box or change the attributes.

The shape highlights the subject of the photo. Optionally, you can add type and then flatten the layers to finish the design for use as a greeting card or advertising piece.

TIPS

More Options!
Create a gradient fill with a color from your image. Click the Foreground Color box to open the Color Picker. Move the cursor outside of the Color Picker dialog box and click a color from your image. Click OK to close the dialog box.

Change It Later!
You can save the file with all the layers so that you can change it later. However, if you need a smaller file, click Layer → Flatten Image and then click File → Save As and save the file with a new filename.

Customize It!
Click the top layer with the shape selection. Add a drop shadow or other effect by clicking the Layer Style icon in the Layers palette (fx). Click an effect and click OK to close the dialog box.

ACCENTUATE A SKY
easily with a gradient fill layer

You may have a scenic photo in which the sky is a bit dull. The lighting may have called for a different exposure setting, or you may need a neutral density filter or polarizing filter on the camera. Still, you may want to use the photo in an album or a graphic design project. Adding a little blue to darken the sky or adding some black to make a gray sky more foreboding can greatly improve an otherwise boring tourist photo.

Adding a gradient fill layer enables you to easily improve a washed-out blue sky or make a gray sky

look stormy. You can visually adjust the amount of color you add, and because you are using a fill layer, you can go back and increase or decrease the amount of color after you apply it. You can even change the color that you apply to get a different effect or to create a dramatic look. This technique is most effective on a photo with a large sky area and an open horizon.

1 Open an image with a dull gray sky.

2 Click the Default Foreground and Background Colors icon to set the foreground to black.

3 Click the New Fill or Adjustment Layer button.

4 Click Gradient.

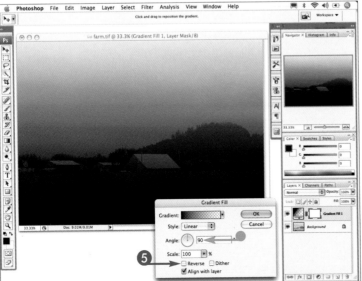

The Gradient Fill dialog box appears, and a foreground-to-transparent gradient is applied to the image.

● Make sure that the angle is set to 90 degrees.

5 Click Reverse.

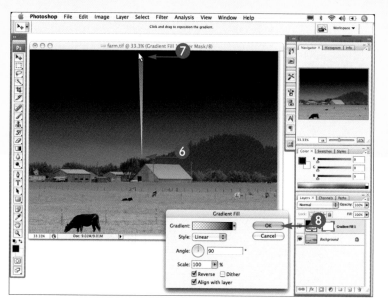

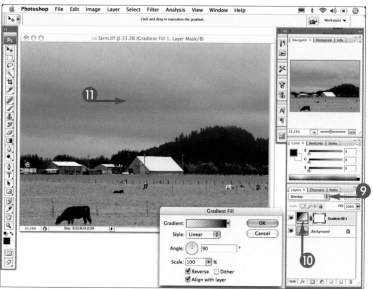

The gradient reverses to black at the top, changing to transparent at the bottom of the image.

⑥ Position the cursor over the image.

⑦ Drag upward in the image until the gradient covers only the sky and the clouds look menacing.

⑧ Click OK.

DIFFICULTY LEVEL

The ominous sky is applied as a layer above the Background layer.

⑨ Click here and select Overlay.

⑩ Double-click the layer thumbnail for the gradient fill.

The Gradient Fill dialog box reappears.

⑪ Repeat steps **6** to **8** to increase or reduce the effect.

Each time that you drag in the image with the Gradient Fill layer selected, the look of the sky changes.

TIPS

More Options!

If your image has a gray sky that requires more drama, set the foreground color in the toolbox to black. If the sky in your photo is blue, set the foreground color in the toolbox to a dark blue before you apply the gradient fill layer. You can even accentuate a sunset by using a reddish-orange color as the foreground color.

Did You Know?

Multiple layers increase the file size of your image. Because Photoshop requires more memory to work on larger files, you should merge layers that will not be adjusted later. Pressing ⌘+E (Ctrl+E) merges the highlighted layer with the layer below. Pressing ⌘+Shift+E (Ctrl+Shift+E) merges all the visible layers.

Using the
QUICK SELECTION TOOL AND
REFINE EDGE PALETTE for selections

Photoshop CS3 introduces a new selection tool enabling you to quickly select broad areas of an image by simply painting them. Using the Quick Selection tool, you can brush over areas to select them, varying the brush size as you work to select difficult areas. You can also just click areas for a more limited selection. You can add to selections by pressing the Shift key and subtract from the selection by holding the Option (Alt) key as you paint.

The new Refine Edge floating palette is accessible in the Options bar whenever any selection tool is selected. Using Refine Edge, you can clean up selections, soften or feather the edge outlines, remove edge artifacts or jaggies, and expand or contract selected areas with more control than by using any of the selection tools alone. The palette offers various previewing options, showing the selection on different backgrounds to help you see the edges of the areas you are selecting and the changes you are making.

1 Click the Quick Selection tool.

2 Click here.

3 Click and drag the Diameter slider to change the brush tip size.

● If you have a Wacom tablet attached, you can use the Size drop-down list to adjust the brush size with pen pressure.

Note: You can press ⌘ (Ctrl)+ spacebar and click to zoom in for more accurate selections.

4 Click and drag inside the part of the image you want to select.

5 Click and drag in another area.

● The selection changes to the Add To option.

6 Press Option (Alt) and click in areas to remove them from the selection.

Note: You can press Option (Alt)+ spacebar and click to zoom out.

7 Click Refine Edge.

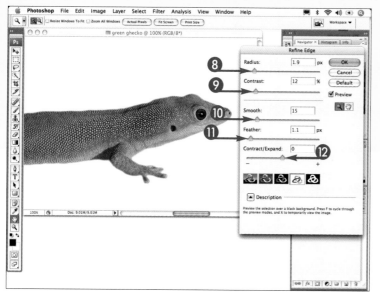

The Refine Edge dialog box appears.

8 Click and drag the Radius slider to the right to soften the edge outline.

9 Click and drag the Contrast slider to the right to remove edge artifacts.

10 Click and drag the Smooth slider to smooth the outline of the selection.

11 Click and drag the Feather slider to create a softer-edged transition from the selection to the surrounding areas.

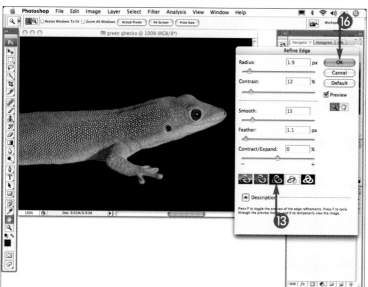

12 Click and drag the Contract/Expand slider to adjust the selection edges.

13 Click a different preview icon to view the selection on a different background.

14 Repeat step **13** to change backgrounds for a better view.

15 Repeat steps **8** to **12** to adjust the selection.

16 Click OK the save the selection adjustments.

Your refined selection appears on the image.

Did You Know?

You can use the Refine Edge palette on any active selection, regardless of the tool used to create the selection. Click Select → Refine Edge when there is any selection in the image. You can also use the palette on any active layer mask to adjust it as it is applied to a layer.

Try This!

You can quickly change the preview background of your selection when using the Refine Edge palette by pressing F. The preview changes each time you press F, cycling through each mode.

Customize It!

When using the Quick Selection tool, you can click the Auto-Enhance option in the Options bar to reduce the roughness of the selection boundary. Depending on the speed of your computer, adding the Auto-Enhance option may slow the selection process.

Using a
QUICK MASK
to make a detailed selection

You can make selections in many different ways in Photoshop CS3. You can select a rectangular or oval area with the Marquee tools, select freeform or geometric areas with the Lasso tools, or use the Magic Wand tool to select similarly colored areas.

You can also use the Quick Selection tool as shown in Task #16 to select specific areas and add to or subtract from selections; however, some images can still require a more detailed or precise selection tool. Using the Brush tool in the Quick Mask mode, you can make a detailed selection or adjust any

previously selected area.

The Quick Mask mode is an editing mode in which protected areas are covered with a translucent colored mask. Painting with the default red color directly on the areas you want can make selecting detail more precise, while enabling you to see what you are selecting. Using this masking technique, you are actually masking the areas you paint, so you must inverse the selection before making any adjustments. The areas you painted in are then selected, and the rest is now masked.

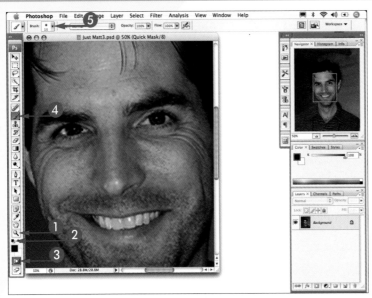

① Click the Zoom tool and click to enlarge the area you want to select.

② Click the Default Colors button to set the foreground color to black and the background to white.

③ Click the Quick Mask mode button.

④ Click the Brush tool.

⑤ Click here.

⑥ Select a hard-edged brush.

⑦ Click and drag to adjust the Master Diameter slider.

⑧ Paint over the areas you want to select.

● The painted areas are covered with a red translucent mask.

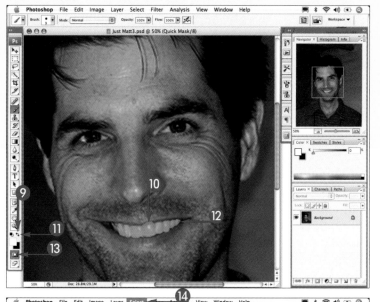

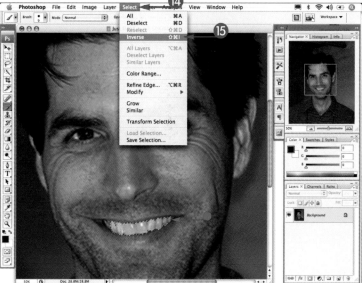

9 Click the Switch Foreground and Background Colors icon to make white the foreground color.

10 Paint over any areas that you covered accidentally.

11 Click the Switch Foreground and Background Colors icon again to make black the foreground color.

12 Continue painting the area to select until the whole area is covered in red.

13 Click here to turn off the Quick Mask mode.

● Dashed lines indicate the area that was masked by the red color.

14 Click Select.

15 Click Inverse.

The selection now includes only the area you painted in the Quick Mask mode.

17

DIFFICULTY LEVEL

Did You Know?

To change the brush size quickly, press the right bracket (]) to increase the paintbrush diameter and the left bracket ([) to reduce it. To toggle the foreground and background colors, press X.

Important!

You may need to feather a selection before you make adjustments. Click Select → Modify → Feather and type a feather value. For the selection of the teeth, use a 1- or 2-pixel feather. You can also click Select → Refine Edge and adjust the selection as shown in Task #16.

More Options!

If the image you are painting on is very red, change the masking color. Double-click the Quick Mask Mode icon and click the color box in the Quick Mask Options dialog box to pick a new color.

EXTRACT THE MAIN SUBJECT
from the background

You will often want to separate a person or an object from the background so that you can use the person or object on a separate layer or in another image. You could painstakingly paint over the person or object with a brush in the Quick Mask mode or select the area with another selection tool; however, the Extract filter may make a better selection, especially for delicate or detailed areas, such as trees or hair.

When you use the Extract filter, Photoshop erases the background of the selected area and makes it

transparent. The filter looks for contrasting edges under the area you highlight. For pixels on the edges, it removes any color derived from the background to avoid having an edge halo when the item is placed on another background.

Although it is a sophisticated tool, the Extract filter may leave some areas that need to be touched up before your selection is complete. You can refine and fix the extraction with another layer and other Photoshop tools.

Photo © 2007 www.photospin.com

1. Open a photo with a subject that you want to extract from the background.

2. Duplicate the Background layer as shown in Task #11.

3. Click here to turn the visibility off for the original Background layer.

4. Click Filter.

5. Click Extract.

   The Extract dialog box opens with your image in the window.

6. Click the Edge Highlighter tool.

7. Click here and move the slider to adjust the brush size.

8. Trace around the edges of the areas that you want to keep.

   Note: Make sure that the marker border is half covering the item that you want to select and half over the background.

9. Click the Fill tool.

10. Click in the area you want to keep.

    The green highlighted area fills with a translucent blue.

11. Click Preview.

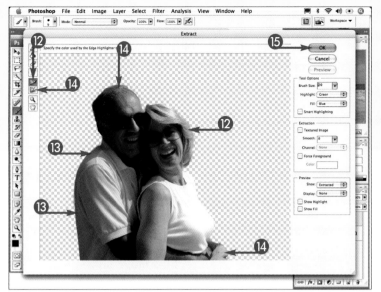

The extracted area appears on a transparent background.

12 Click the Clean Up tool and draw around any ragged edges to remove excess background.

13 Hold the Option (Alt) key down and paint in the image to fill in any areas that dropped out.

14 Click the Edge Touchup tool and draw around any rough edges to clean them up.

15 Click OK.

● The selected area is extracted.

16 Press ⌘+J (Ctrl+J) to duplicate the layer.

Note: Duplicating the layer generally fixes other dropped-out areas.

17 Press ⌘+E (Ctrl+E) to merge the two extracted layers.

The subject of the photo is extracted on a separate layer. You can now drag that layer into another photo or change the background behind the subject by adding a different layer below the subject layer.

DIFFICULTY LEVEL

TIPS

Caution!
If the blue fill color spills into the rest of the image, your subject was not completely enclosed by the highlight border. Press ⌘+Z (Ctrl+Z) to undo and outline the edge completely before filling.

More Options!
Use a small brush to highlight well-defined areas and a larger brush to highlight wispy areas, such as hair. Pressing the left ([) or right (]) bracket keys changes the brush sizes quickly, as you highlight the object.

Try This!
To preview the extraction against a plain background, click the Display drop-down menu in the Preview palette on the right. Select Gray Matte or any other color that makes it easy to see your selection.

Open or add layers as
SMART OBJECTS
for nondestructive changes

A *smart object layer* is a different type of layer, acting as a pointer to the original image file and giving you complete creative flexibility when editing any image. For example, if you drag a photograph to copy it into another document as a regular layer, the layer adopts the characteristics of the base image. When you use the Transformation command to make the image smaller, the dimensions of the image on the layer are reduced. If you later want to increase the size of the image on that layer, you lose image quality because your previous transformation

removed pixels to reduce the size. If instead you open the same photograph as a smart object layer, you can continuously transform the layer without any image data loss.

You can open a document as a smart object, place a file into another document as a smart object, or convert one or more already open Photoshop layers to smart objects. You can also place an Illustrator or other vector file into a document as a smart object and maintain the vector's sharp edges or forms even when resizing.

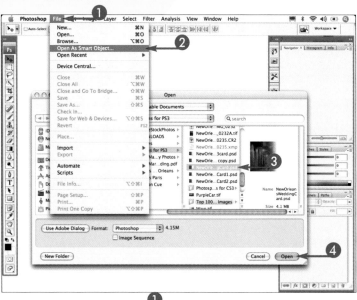

OPEN AN IMAGE AS A SMART OBJECT

1. Click File.

2. Click Open As Smart Object.

   The Open dialog box appears.

3. Navigate to and click a file to open.

4. Click Open.

   The file opens as a smart object.

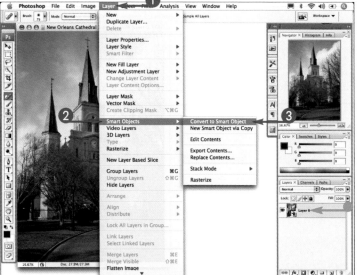

CONVERT AN OPEN IMAGE LAYER TO A SMART OBJECT LAYER

1. With an image already open, click Layer.

2. Click Smart Objects.

3. Click Convert to Smart Object.

   ● The layer is changed to a smart object layer and appears in the Layers palette with the Smart Object icon. The layer is also renamed to Layer 0.

42

① Open the file where the Illustrator document will be placed.

② Click File.

③ Click Place.

The Open dialog box appears.

④ Navigate to and click an Illustrator file to open.

⑤ Click Place in the Open dialog box.

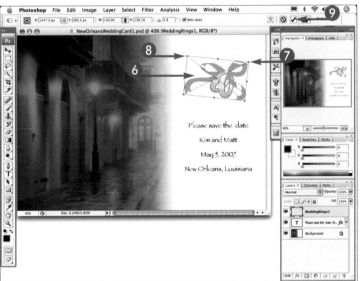

The image appears inside a box with an *X* through it.

⑥ Click in the placed file and drag it to a new location.

⑦ Click and drag the bounding box anchors to resize the smart object.

⑧ Click and drag just outside one of the corners to rotate the file.

⑨ Click here to apply the placed image.

The box is removed from the image and a new smart object layer appears above the previous layer in the Layers palette.

TIPS

More Options!

Click Layer → Smart Objects → Edit Contents. Click OK in the warning dialog box that appears. Edit the original file that appears and press ⌘+S (Ctrl+S), and the smart object image is updated. Or just double-click directly on the Smart Object icon on the layer thumbnail to alter the original image.

Try This!

You can create duplicates of a smart object layer in a document and link them. When you replace the contents of one smart object layer, all the duplicates are automatically updated at the same time.

Did You Know?

You can place a camera RAW image from the Bridge as a smart object layer into a Photoshop file. The smart object layer remains completely editable as a camera RAW file without any data loss.

Apply filters as
SMART FILTERS
for dynamic adjustments

After you have a smart object layer, you can add smart filters. This new type of filter is completely nondestructive and offers more image-editing flexibility than ever before.

Actually, any filter applied to a smart object layer becomes a smart filter. Compared to normal filters, smart filters offer adjustments without compromising any pixel data. You can remove or hide smart filters

at any time. In addition, you can continuously edit the settings of the smart filters to achieve different effects. You can add multiple filters one on top of one another. You can change the order of the smart filters to change the resulting effect. When you add a mask to a smart filter, you can paint in the mask to hide or reveal different areas of the filter for refined edits, all without altering the image data.

① Open an image as a smart object as shown in Task #19.

② Click Filter.

③ Click the filter that you want.

④ Click the type of change you want to make with the filter.

The filter's dialog box appears.

⑤ Click and drag the sliders and adjust other options as needed.

⑥ Click OK.

● The smart filter appears below the smart object layer in the Layers palette.

⑦ Click Filter.

⑧ Click another filter to apply to the image.

The filter's dialog box appears.

⑨ Repeat steps **5** and **6**.

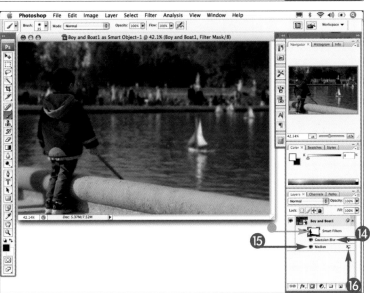

DIFFICULTY LEVEL

- The second smart filter appears above the first.

⑩ Click the mask thumbnail.

⑪ Click the Brush tool.

⑫ Click here and select a soft-edge brush with a size to fit your image.

- Make sure that the default foreground color is black. Press D to restore the default and X if necessary to make the foreground color black.

⑬ Paint in the image where you do not want the filters applied.

Note: For example, the smart filters here blur the background. You paint with black to remove the blur from the main subject.

- The painted areas appear black in the Smart Filters effects mask, and the filters are removed from those areas in the photo.

⑭ Click here and drag the second smart filter below the first to see if the effect is preferable.

⑮ Click here to turn on and off the Visibility icons of the individual smart filters to see the before and after effects.

⑯ Double-click here to open the individual Smart Filter dialog boxes and readjust the settings.

TIPS

Did You Know?

Only the Extract, Liquify, Pattern Maker, and Vanishing Point filters cannot be used as smart filters. The Shadow/ Highlight and the Variations adjustments can be applied as smart filters with a smart object layer.

Try This!

Click the triangle by the smart object layer to display the smart filters applied to the layer. Double-click the two triangle arrows next to the smart filter to change the blending mode and opacity of the smart filter.

More Options!

To delete an individual smart filter, click its name and drag it to the Layers palette Trash. To delete all the smart filters on a layer at once, click and drag the text "Smart Filters" on the smart object layer to the Trash.

Straightening, Cropping, and Resizing

A well-balanced image, free from odd-looking distortions, can mean the difference between a snapshot and a good photograph. The overall layout of the image, how it is cropped, and where the main subject is placed in relation to the background are important in both design and photography. A crooked horizon or unbalanced subject matter can make even a great image look like the work of a beginner. You may have buildings that appear top heavy or out of perspective, and your photos will not always be the size you need them for your projects. Even the best photographers have images that require some cropping or resizing.

With Photoshop CS3, you can crop images for better composition with a variety of tools and straighten the horizon in any photo. You can also straighten and crop several crookedly scanned photos in one step. You can even make multiple photos from one original image or create a panorama from several separate images. You can fix various types of camera lens distortions and correct the perspective on buildings. Photoshop and Camera Raw do most of the work for you.

Photoshop CS3 makes all such previously time-consuming or difficult tasks quick and easy. New tools and new resampling algorithms help you straighten, crop, adjust, and resize images, saving hours of tedious work to make all your images look better.

Top 100

CROP YOUR IMAGES
and use a rule-of-thirds grid to improve composition

Designers and photographers use various techniques to balance an image and catch the viewer's attention. They may change the placement of the horizon to the upper or lower third of the image. They may divide the entire image into thirds horizontally and vertically and place the main subject at the intersection of the thirds. They may just offset the main subject to guide the viewer into the image. Perfectly composing a photograph in the camera's viewfinder is not always possible; however, you can recompose and improve that photo by cropping it in Photoshop.

You can use Photoshop's rulers and drag guides to divide the image into thirds as guidelines or just to mark the center of focus as a visual reference. With your image on a separate layer, you can use the Move tool to recompose your image, placing the main subject where it is most effective.

Then you can use the Crop tool to crop the image with your new composition. You can also crop visually, specify dimensions in the Options bar, use one of the preset sizes, or create a crop size and save it as a preset.

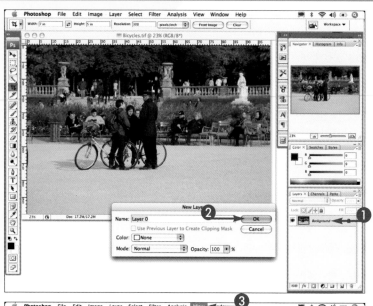

1 With the image you want to crop opened, double-click the Background layer's name.

The New Layer dialog box appears with a new name for the layer.

2 Click OK.

The locked Background layer changes to a regular layer.

3 Click View.

4 Click New Guide.

The New Guide dialog box appears with Vertical selected.

5 Type **33%** in the Position box.

6 Click OK.

A vertical blue guide appears on the first third of the image.

⑦ Repeat steps **3** to **6**, typing **66%** in step **5**.

A second vertical blue guide appears on the second third of the image.

⑧ Click View.

⑨ Click New Guide.

⑩ Click Horizontal in the New Guide dialog box.

⑪ Type **33%** in the Position box.

⑫ Click OK.

⑬ Repeat steps **8** to **12**, typing **66%** in step **11**.

A rule-of-thirds grid is visible over the image.

⑭ Click the Move tool.

⑮ Click and drag in the image to place the main focus of the image into a third or near an intersection of two guides.

⑯ Click the Crop tool.

⑰ Click and drag in the image to select your image.

⑱ Click here to accept the crop.

● You can click View → Clear Guides to remove the guides.

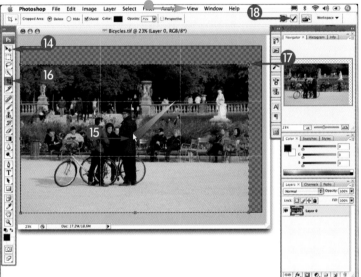

TIPS

Try This!
You can use the Crop tool to rotate the area and get a different composition. Drag out a marquee with the Crop tool. Then move the cursor just outside the area. It changes to a double-headed arrow. The crop rotates as you move the cursor. Click the Commit button to commit the crop.

Customize It!
Create your own Crop tool preset. Click the Crop tool and type your values in the Options bar. Click the Tool Preset Picker, the leftmost thumbnail in the Options bar. Click the New Tool Preset icon on the right in the drop-down menu. Name your tool in the dialog box and click OK. Your custom cropping tool is added to the menu.

Create a
LEVEL HORIZON

You may have a photograph that is perfect for your design, but the photo was shot at a crooked angle. You can easily fix that photograph in Photoshop without doing any math to adjust the angle of the horizon line.

Photoshop includes a Ruler tool, found in the toolbox under the Eyedropper tool. This tool is intended to help you position elements precisely in a design layout and can calculate distances between two points in the unit of measure that you have set in

Preferences. When you click and drag the tool across your image, a nonprinting line is drawn, and the Options bar displays all the numeric information relating to the line and angle.

You can also use this tool to have Photoshop calculate how many degrees your image should be rotated to level the horizon and then have Photoshop straighten the photo for you. You can then use the Crop tool to cut off the angled edges of the image, giving your photograph a straight horizon line.

① In an image that needs a level horizon line, click and hold the Eyedropper tool to reveal the Ruler tool.

② Click the Ruler tool.

③ Click and drag from one side of the image to the other, along what should be a horizontal plane or the horizon line.

● The Ruler tool draws a line across the image.

④ Click Image.

⑤ Click Rotate Canvas.

⑥ Click Arbitrary.

The Rotate Canvas dialog box opens with the exact angle needed to straighten the horizon.

⑦ Click OK.

The image is rotated, and the horizon is more level.

⑧ Click the Crop tool.

⑨ Click and drag in the image to select the area that you want to crop.

⑩ Drag the corner anchors to the edges.

⑪ Drag the center anchors up or down to fit the image.

⑫ Click the Commit button in the Options bar to commit the crop.

The image is cropped, and the horizon is now straight.

TIPS

Did You Know?

You can easily check the dimensions of an open photo without opening the Image Size dialog box. Select the Crop tool and click Front Image in the Options bar. The current width, height, and resolution are shown in the data fields.

Attention!

The Crop tool retains the dimensions of the previous crop. Be sure to click Clear in the Options bar to reset the tool and remove any old settings before you click and drag the Crop marquee in a new image.

Try This!

Although you have less control over the area to be cropped, you can crop a photo using the Rectangular Marquee tool. Click and drag a selection in the image with the Marquee tool. Click Image → Crop.

TRY A REVERSE CROP
to expand the canvas

When you think of cropping, you generally think of reducing the physical size of an image by cutting away areas around the borders. In Photoshop, you can also use the Crop tool to expand your canvas, give your photo or image a wider border, or quickly create a new colored background for a photo.

Although using the Canvas Size menu and dialog box is more precise, expanding the canvas with the Crop tool is quick, and you can see exactly how your enlarged canvas appears. In addition, using the reverse-crop method, you can create a border that is

uneven, larger on one side than the other for a page layout, or larger on the bottom than on the top as in a gallery print.

You can use this technique to enlarge your canvas visually or with precise dimensions for your final image. If you are working on a series of images with specific sizes, you can create a custom Crop tool preset and then use that tool to quickly reverse crop the photos. All your images have the same-sized canvas, making your design and layout tasks much easier.

① In an opened image, click the Default Color icon in the toolbox to set the foreground to black and the background to white.

② Click the Zoom tool.

③ Click the Zoom Out box in the Options bar.

④ Click in the image several times to zoom out.

The image view becomes smaller on a gray background area.

⑤ Click the Crop tool.

⑥ Click and drag across the entire image.

● The crop marquee surrounds the image.

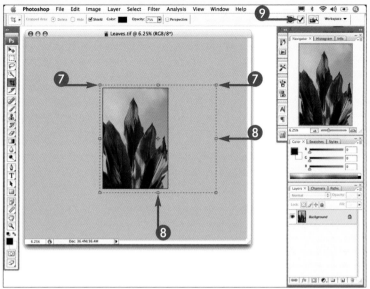

7 Click and drag on the corner anchor points of the crop marquee to extend the crop area.

8 Click and drag on the center anchor points until the borders fit your design.

9 Click the Commit button in the Options bar to commit the crop.

● The canvas is enlarged and filled with the default background color.

TIPS

More Options!
You can use the technique shown here to quickly create a gift tag or a note card. Enlarge the canvas as shown in the task steps, click the Type tool, and type some text in the white canvas area.

Try This!
Click the Background Color box in the toolbox and select another color. When you enlarge the canvas using the reverse-crop method, the area will fill with your selected color instead of white.

Change It!
Click the Crop tool and type the width and height for your finished design in the boxes in the Options bar. When you click and drag out the crop marquee in the image, it maintains the exact dimensions you typed.

CROP AND STRAIGHTEN
in Camera Raw

Many digital cameras can save image files in the Camera Raw format. Camera Raw image files are digital negatives and contain the actual picture data from the digital camera's image sensor without any in-camera processing applied. Photographers often prefer editing in Camera Raw to maintain more control because they can interpret the image data rather than let the camera make the adjustments and conversions automatically.

Photoshop CS3 not only enables you to make color and sharpness enhancements to a variety of Raw

formats as well as JPEGs and TIFFs, but you can also crop and straighten those images in Camera Raw before opening them in Photoshop.

After you crop and straighten the image files in the Camera Raw dialog box, you can save them in Camera Raw and reprocess the file at any time with maximum control. You can also continue to edit and refine them in Photoshop and save them in a standard file format.

Using Camera Raw to crop and straighten gives you more options for editing and saving images.

① Launch the Bridge and click a JPEG, TIFF, or Raw format image.

② Click File.

③ Click Open in Camera Raw.

The photo opens in the Camera Raw dialog box.

Note: If the file is already in a Raw format, you can open it with Photoshop CS3, which automatically opens it in the Camera Raw dialog box.

④ Click the Straighten tool.

⑤ Click and drag on a horizontal or vertical line in the preview image.

● The preview image is rotated with the new angle, and a maximum bounding box appears.

● The Crop tool is automatically selected.

⑥ Click and drag the corner anchors to adjust the composition of the photo if necessary.

⑦ Click and drag inside the bounding box to move the entire selection in the image.

The bounding box moves to the area of the photograph that you want.

⑧ Press and hold Option (Alt).

● The Open Image button changes to Open Copy.

⑨ Click Open Copy to open the image in Photoshop without altering your original.

Note: *Holding the Option (Alt) key down also changes the Cancel button to Reset so that you can start over.*

The cropped and straightened image opens in Photoshop.

TIPS

Did You Know?

You can apply the same cropping dimensions to multiple images. Open the images in Camera Raw. Click Select All on the left of the dialog box. Click Synchronize and select the Crop check box in the Synchronize dialog box. Click OK to close the dialog box. Select the Crop tool and crop the topmost image. All selected images are cropped in the same way.

More Options!

You can make a crop with specific proportions in Camera Raw. Click and hold the Crop tool to reveal the pop-up menu. Click one of the presets or click Custom. In the Custom Crop dialog box, type the exact proportions or dimensions that you need and click OK. The Crop tool is set for your specific size.

STRAIGHTEN CROOKED SCANS
quickly

When you are not bogged down with repetitive tasks, you can be more productive and creative. Photoshop has many features to help both your productivity and your creativity, such as automated image processing.

Scanning images one by one is one of those redundant projects that can be very time-consuming. You have to scan one image, crop it, and save it — and then lift the scanner top, reposition another image on the scanner bed, and start over.

Using a flat bed scanner with a large scanning area, such as Microtek's i800, you can scan multiple

images at one time and let Photoshop separate these into multiple files. Photoshop's automation tool also saves time when scanning just one photo. You can place a photo on the scanner bed without lining it up perfectly because Photoshop's Crop and Straighten Photos command can crop and straighten that one scan.

The Crop and Straighten Photos command works best when the images have clearly defined edges and there is at least 1/8 inch between each image. The command may work more quickly if all the images have similar tones.

Photo of boy © 2007
www.photospin.com

① In Photoshop, open a file with multiple scans.

② Click File.

③ Click Automate.

④ Click Crop and Straighten Photos.

A progress bar appears as Photoshop separates and crops each image in the file.

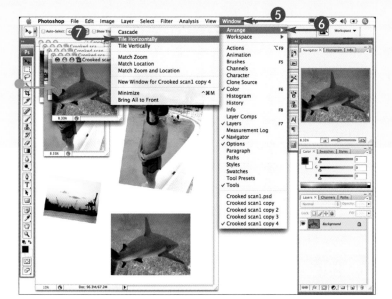

- Each image is opened in its own window.

5 Click Window.

6 Click Arrange.

7 Click Tile Horizontally (or Tile Vertically).

DIFFICULTY LEVEL

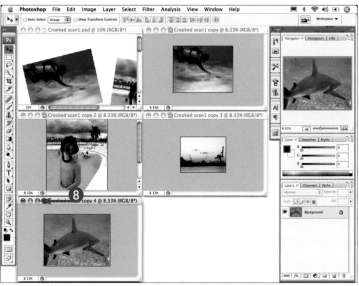

Photoshop arranges the original scan and all the separate images on the screen.

8 Click the Zoom (Maximize) button to view each image at full size.

TIPS

Important!

Photoshop does not replace the original scan with the separated photos, and it does not automatically save the separate images. Instead, Photoshop renames each separated file using the same name as the original scan and labeling it "copy," "copy 2," and so on. You can click File ➔ Save As and rename each file before you save it.

More Options!

You may scan multiple images at once and decide that you want to keep only one of them. Make a selection border around that one image, including some background. Press and hold Option (Alt) as you select File ➔ Automate ➔ Crop and Straighten Photos. Photoshop crops and straightens that one photo and puts it in a separate file.

CROP MULTIPLE IMAGES
from one original to create a triptych

Although tools such as the Crop and Straighten Photos command are meant as productivity aids to crop and straighten multiple images at one time, you can use the same tool in various creative ways.

You can create multiple images from one file by using the command to divide one photograph into multiple sections. You can make individual photographs from each section of the original or apply a diptych or triptych look to an image, making two or three panels for the image, which you can print and frame separately.

Select a plain, rectangular frame shape as a custom shape to designate the areas that you want to crop into new images. Photoshop turns those separate shapes into separate images that you can save as new files. The trick to this technique is to leave a small margin around each of the shape selections and to create a separate layer for each shape when you use the Custom Shape tool. You can use the shape as part of your final print, or you can delete it because it is on a separate layer.

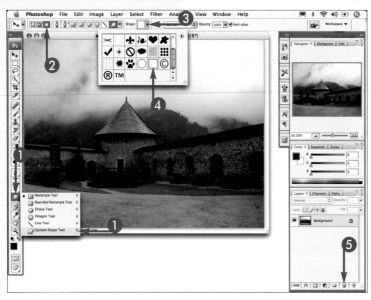

① In a large file, click and hold the Rectangle tool and select the Custom Shape tool.

② Click the Fill Pixels icon in the Options bar.

③ Click here.

④ Select the square thin frame shape.

⑤ Click the New Layer icon in the Layers palette.

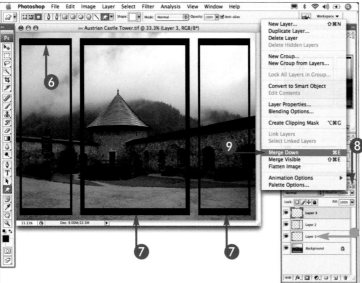

● A new blank layer is placed above the background.

⑥ Click and drag a frame shape in the image.

⑦ Repeat steps **5** and **6** twice to have two more layers and two more frame shapes.

Note: Keep at least a 1/8 inch space between each shape.

⑧ Click here.

⑨ Click Merge Down.

10 Repeat steps **8** and **9** so that there is only one layer above the Background layer.

11 Click File.

12 Click Automate.

13 Click Crop and Straighten Photos.

#26

DIFFICULTY LEVEL

Photoshop separates the segments and creates three new files with the name of the original plus "copy," "copy 2," and "copy 3."

14 Click the Close button of the original file.

15 Click the Maximize button on each of the three new files to enlarge them.

16 Click and drag each file to align the three new separate files to view the triptych.

TIPS

Caution!
Be sure to create a new layer for each frame that you draw. You can then resize and rotate the shapes by clicking Edit → Free Transform and transforming the frame shape with the transformation anchors. Before you apply the Crop and Straighten Photos command, merge all the custom shape layers into one layer above the original image.

More Options!
Each image has a shape layer above the photo layer. You can drag the shape layer to the Trash to remove it, or you can use the shape to add a framed look. Press ⌘ (Ctrl) + click the shape layer to select it. Click Edit → Fill and select a new color for the frames. Then click Layer → Layer Style and apply a bevel and drop shadow to the shape layer.

CHANGE YOUR PERSPECTIVE
with the Crop tool

When you photograph an object from an angle rather than from a straight-on view, the object appears out of perspective, displaying keystone distortion. The top edges of a tall building photographed from ground level appear closer to each other at the top than they do at the bottom. If you photograph a window and cannot get directly in front of it to take the shot, the window appears more like a trapezoid. Depending on the photograph, you can correct this type of distortion with a number of Photoshop's tools.

The Crop tool in Photoshop CS3 has a special option that enables you to transform the perspective in an image and quickly adjust the keystone distortion. Your image must have an object that was rectangular in the original scene for the Crop tool's perspective function to work properly. You first adjust the cropping marquee to match the rectangular object's edges and then extend the marquee to fit your image. When you click the Commit button, Photoshop crops the image as large as possible while maintaining the angles of the rectangular object.

1 In a photo containing a distorted rectangular object, click the Crop tool.

2 Click Clear in the Options bar to remove any previous settings.

3 Click and drag a cropping marquee in the image.

   The selected area is light, and the area that you want to crop away is dimmed.

4 Click here to deselect Shield to remove the dimming effect.

5 Click here to select Perspective.

6 Click each corner anchor of the cropping marquee and align it with a corner on a normally rectangular object.

   Note: *To zoom in with the crop marquee showing, press ⌘+spacebar (Ctrl+spacebar) and click in the image. Press Option+spacebar (Alt+spacebar) and click in the image to zoom out.*

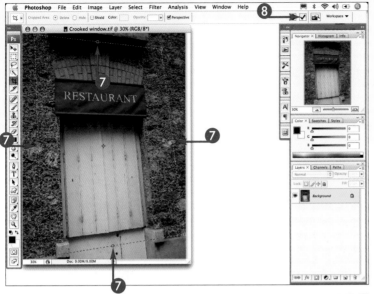

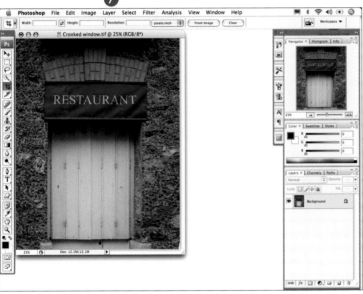

7 Click and drag out each of the center anchor points to fit the edges of the entire image.

8 Click the Commit button in the Options bar to commit the crop.

DIFFICULTY LEVEL

Photoshop realigns the image and changes the perspective.

TIPS

Caution!

Photoshop's Crop tool will not work to correct keystoning on all images. The Crop tool may not fix the perspective distortion if it is applied to an image that has already been cropped for size.

Keyboard Shortcuts!

Press C to access the Crop tool. Press Return (Enter) to commit the perspective crop or Esc to cancel it. Or press Control+click (right-click) in the image and select Crop or Cancel from the menu.

Attention!

If Photoshop shows an error, you may not have placed the corner handles correctly. Click the Cancel button in the Options bar and adjust the cropping marquee before clicking the Commit button and committing the crop.

STRAIGHTEN BUILDINGS
with the Lens Correction filter

Depending on the focal length of a camera lens or the f-stop used, a photograph may show common lens flaws such as barrel and pincushion distortion. Barrel distortion causes straight lines to bow out toward the edges of the image. Pincushion distortion is the opposite effect, where straight lines bend inward. If the camera tilts up or down or at any angle, the perspective also appears distorted. The Lens Correction filter in Photoshop CS3 can help you fix these and other lens defects easily.

When you photograph tall buildings, the tops of the buildings may appear to be larger at the top than the bottom. The Lens Correction filter enables you to easily line up the perspective of the buildings with a vertical plane. You can use the filter's image grid to make your adjustments more accurately, or you can turn the grid off if you choose. The filter even has an option to let you select how to correct the missing areas along the edges that occurred when the perspective was repaired.

① Open an image showing a tall distorted building as a smart object or open a file and convert it to a smart object layer.

Note: *See Task #19 for information about smart objects.*

② Click Filter.

③ Click Distort.

④ Click Lens Correction.

The Lens Correction dialog box appears with a large preview of the image and a grid overlay.

⑤ Drag the Vertical Perspective slider to align the tallest building with the grid.

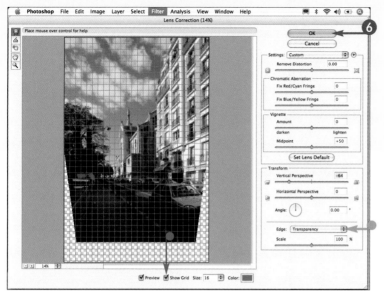

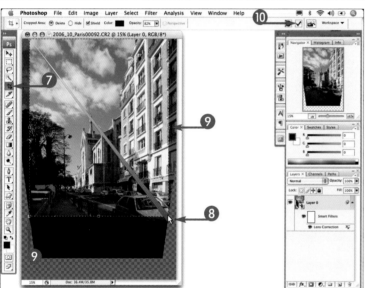

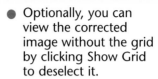

The image appears with a changed perspective plane.

● Optionally, you can view the edge against a dark background by clicking here and selecting Background Color.

● Optionally, you can view the corrected image without the grid by clicking Show Grid to deselect it.

⑥ Click OK to commit the changes.

The adjusted image reopens in Photoshop.

Note: You can edit the adjustment by double-clicking the Lens Correction smart filter in the Layers palette before cropping the final image.

⑦ Click the Crop tool.

⑧ Click and drag in the image.

⑨ Click the anchors of the crop area to adjust your image.

⑩ Click the Commit button in the Options bar.

The image is cropped, and the buildings appear straight.

TIPS

Try This!
You can reset the adjustments in the Lens Correction dialog box by pressing Option (Alt). The Cancel button changes to Reset. Click Reset to remove the changes and start over. You can change Cancel buttons in most dialog boxes to Reset by pressing Option (Alt).

More Options!
You can save the Lens Correction settings and reapply them to other images. Set the options in the dialog box. Click the Manage Settings drop-down arrow and choose Save Settings. The saved settings appear in the Settings drop-down menu.

Did You Know?
In addition to barrel and pincushion distortion, the Lens Correction filter can fix both *chromatic aberration,* a colored fringe along the edges of objects, and *vignetting,* the appearance of darker corners or edges in the image.

Create a
PANORAMA FROM MULTIPLE PHOTOS

You can combine multiple photographs into one continuous image to create a panorama. For example, you can take two or more overlapping photographs of a scenic horizon, or even a number of scans of parts of a large document, and then assemble them in Photoshop with the Photomerge command. You can combine photos that are tiled horizontally as well as vertically.

Although you can also choose to position and blend the images manually using Interactive Layout, the Photomerge command in Photoshop CS3 is more powerful than the previous version, automatically aligning and blending each layer using individual layer masks.

To make the merge as successful as possible, photos or scans intended for merging should have an overlap of 25 percent to 40 percent. Also maintain the same exposure for each photograph and keep the same scanning settings for each scan. Using a tripod to keep the camera level when taking the photos also improves the final merge.

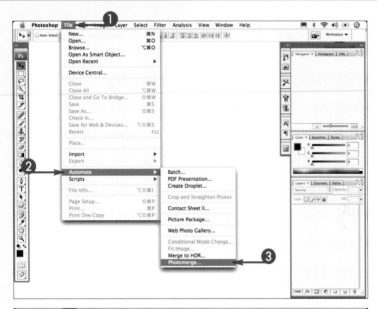

① In Photoshop, click File.

② Click Automate.

③ Click Photomerge.

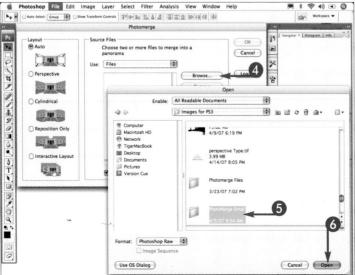

The Photomerge dialog box appears.

④ Click Browse.

The Open dialog box appears.

⑤ Navigate to and select the images to merge.

⑥ Click Open.

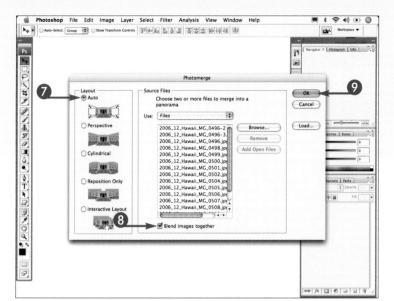

The selected files are listed in the dialog box.

⑦ Click Auto.

⑧ Make sure that Blend Images Together is selected.

⑨ Click OK.

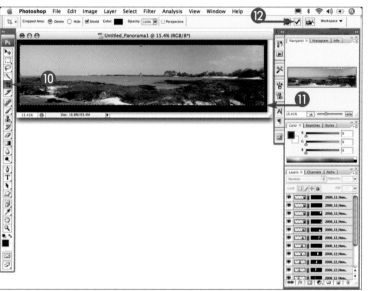

Photoshop aligns the images based on content and blends them into a single image.

Note: The new image is a multilayered file.

⑩ Click the Crop tool.

⑪ Click and drag across the blended image to make your final panorama.

⑫ Click the Commit button in the Options bar.

The panorama is cropped to the selected edges.

TIPS

Did You Know?
When you shoot photos that you intend to merge together, use the Portrait mode rather than Landscape and shoot more images. You will have a larger area to crop from for your final image, giving you a taller and more realistic result.

More Options!
The Perspective option uses one image as a reference and adjusts the perspective of the other images to match and overlap the content of the reference image. The Cylindrical option reduces the bowed shape that can occur in some merged photos.

Change It!
You can add more files by clicking the Browse button again and navigating to add source files. You can always remove a file from the Source Files list by selecting the file and clicking Remove.

MAXIMIZE YOUR IMAGE SIZE
with minimal visible loss

You often need a different size image than the original. You can resize images using the Image Size dialog box.

You can adjust the width, height, or resolution without affecting image quality or pixel dimensions by deselecting the Resample Image check box in the dialog box. However, to change the overall size of an image, you must check the box, and Photoshop resamples by adding or removing pixels to adjust for the changes.

Photoshop's *interpolation methods* — the way that it assigns values to added pixels and smooths transitions between juxtaposing pixels — work well

to preserve the quality and detail as long as the size changes are not extreme. Third-party plug-ins such as onOne's Genuine Fractals and Alien Skin's BlowUp are better for enlarging greater than 150 to 200 percent.

The generally recommended resampling method for reducing image size is Bicubic Sharper, whereas Bicubic Smoother is intended for enlarging. However, many photographers find that depending on the image, the Bicubic Sharper resampling method, along with a resolution of 360 ppi, actually works well both for enlarging and reducing photos.

① With the photo that you want to enlarge open, click Image.

② Click Image Size.

● The size of the image as shown onscreen is visible in this box.

The Image Size dialog box appears, showing the current size of the opened image.

③ Make sure that the Resample Image check box is selected.

④ Double-click in the Width box to highlight all the numbers.

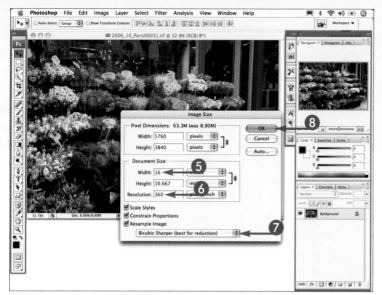

⑤ Type the width that you want for the final printed image.

The height automatically adjusts proportionally.

⑥ Type **360** in the Resolution box.

⑦ Click here and select Bicubic Sharper.

⑧ Click OK.

A progress bar appears as Photoshop processes the enlargement.

The enlarged photo appears.

⑨ Check the file size in the window frame.

TIPS

Test It!

Make two copies of an image. Enlarge the first using Bicubic Smoother and the second using Bicubic Sharper. Crop the same 4-x-6-inch section on both enlargements and paste these into two new documents. Because resampling may reduce detail and sharpness, apply the Smart Sharpen filter with the same settings to each new document and print them for comparison.

Did You Know?

A resolution of 150 to 360 ppi is generally recommended for inkjet printing. Images for onscreen viewing only need a resolution of 72 ppi. Images intended for a printing press require a resolution of twice the line screen of the press. If the line screen is 133 dpi, the resolution should be 266 ppi. Rounding up to 300 ppi is generally recommended.

Chapter 4

Retouching Portraits

You can use Photoshop to give your subjects a digital makeover and make them look more beautiful, younger, and healthier. However, it is so easy to alter images in Photoshop that new users often overdo it and make people look like plastic versions of themselves. You are trying to enhance a person's best features and minimize other areas, not turn him or her into someone else. If your subject looks at his photo and thinks that he looks good, you have done your job well.

You can use Photoshop CS3 for removing blemishes and red eye, enhancing the eyes, reducing wrinkles, whitening teeth, softening the face, and more. You can also change someone's hair color or eye color to fit a client's request. You can add to any portrait by adding a catch light to the eyes, even if it was

not captured by the camera. You can even reduce certain undesirable sags without plastic surgery.

Applying the enhancements on separate layers enables you to preserve the original image as well as blend or reduce the changes, making them appear more natural. You should always work on a duplicate of the original file even when you make minor enhancements. For the final image, select Flatten Image from the Layer menu before saving it with a new name. Just do not show the original unretouched photo to the subject!

Because these enhancements should be subtle, using a pen tablet, such as the Wacom Intuos 3, is particularly useful when retouching portraits.

Top 100

REMOVE BLEMISHES
and improve the skin

You can greatly improve a portrait by removing skin imperfections. Blemishes may be natural, but they are rarely a desirable feature in a photograph. With Photoshop, you can easily remove or reduce the number of blemishes. You can even leave some but make them less obvious.

With previous versions of Photoshop, you could use the Clone Stamp tool or the Patch tool for this task. Photoshop CS introduced the Healing Brush, which is even better for repairing certain skin imperfections.

The Spot Healing Brush is now the simplest tool to use for removing blemishes. This tool automatically samples the areas around the spot to be removed and blends the pixels. The key to using the Spot Healing Brush is to choose a brush size that is just slightly larger than the blemish and to work in stages on separate layers.

You can then change the opacity of each layer and make the changes less obvious. If you do not like the changes, you can simply discard the layers.

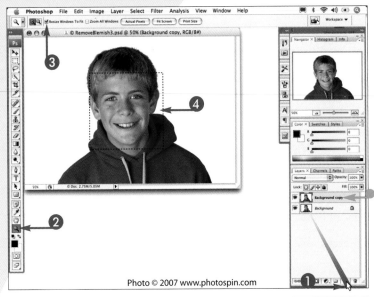

Photo © 2007 www.photospin.com

① With the image open, drag the Background layer over the New Layer icon to duplicate it.

● A Background copy layer is added, but the screen does not change.

② Click the Zoom tool.

③ Click Resize Windows To Fit.

④ Click and drag over the blemish areas to zoom in.

The image is enlarged and fills the screen.

⑤ Click the New Layer icon to add a new blank layer.

● A new layer is added in the Layers palette, but the screen does not change.

⑥ Click the Spot Healing Brush.

⑦ Click Sample All Layers.

⑧ Click here to open the Brush Picker.

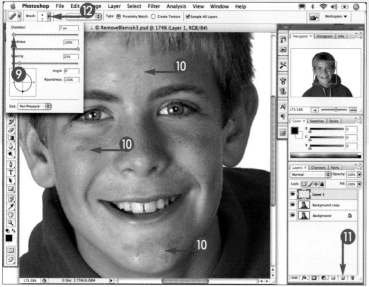

9 Click and drag the Diameter slider to adjust the brush size.

Note: *The brush size should be just larger than the blemish that you want to remove.*

10 Click each of the worst blemishes of a similar size first.

Photoshop removes the blemishes and blends the surrounding skin area.

11 Click the New Layer icon to add another blank layer.

12 Repeat steps **8** to **10**, clicking the other blemishes.

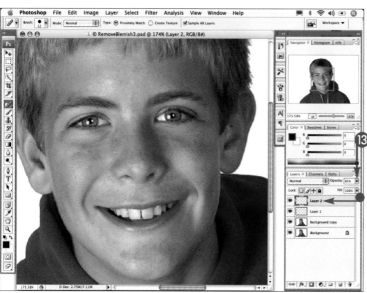

● Layer 2 should be highlighted in the Layers palette.

13 Click here and drag the Opacity slider for Layer 2 to the left until the skin looks natural.

31

DIFFICULTY LEVEL

TIPS

Attention!
Moles, freckles, or other distinguishing marks are a distinct feature. Unlike most blemishes, these permanent marks may be considered essential to the person's character. Be sure to check with the subject or the art director first before removing these.

More Options!
After removing the blemishes, you can combine the blemish repair layers with the Background copy layer. You can quickly compare the before and after images by turning on and off the Visibility icon for the Background copy layer.

Did You Know?
With a pen tablet, you can set the size in the Brush Picker to Pen Pressure and set the brush size to be larger than the largest blemish. Press harder to remove large blemishes and press lightly to remove smaller blemishes.

REMOVE BLEMISHES
and improve the skin

The Spot Healing Brush generally removes blemishes and imperfections and makes the skin appear cleaner. However, the blemishes often discolor the surrounding skin tone, and removing the blemishes can leave spots or streaks of mismatched colors on your subject. You can easily improve the overall skin tone and smooth any blotches the Healing Brush may have left using the skin-smoothing technique, as taught by Jane Conner-ziser.

Known as one of the best photo retouchers in the professional photography industry, Jane teaches

classes in portrait photography, facial retouching, and fine-art portrait painting at her Digital Art School in Florida, as well as across the United States and internationally. You can learn more about Jane's many classes and seminars at janesdigitalart.com.

This technique adds a special dodge and burn layer to your image. You can control the amount of tonal adjustment and improve the skin without making the photo appear retouched and without altering your original file.

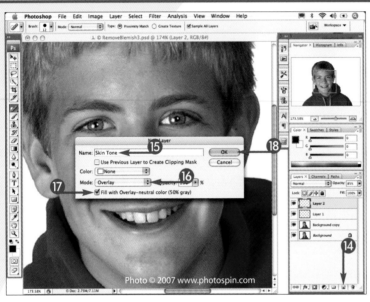

Photo © 2007 www.photospin.com

⓮ Press the Option key and click the New Layer icon.

The New Layer dialog box appears.

⓯ Type a name such as **Skin Tone** in the Name field.

⓰ Click here and select Overlay for the mode.

⓱ Click Fill with Overlay-Neutral Color (50% Gray).

⓲ Click OK.

● A gray layer in Overlay mode appears in the Layers palette.

⓳ Click the Brush tool.

⓴ Click here and select a small soft-edged brush.

㉑ Click here and reduce the brush opacity to about 3%.

㉒ Click here to reset the default colors to black and white.

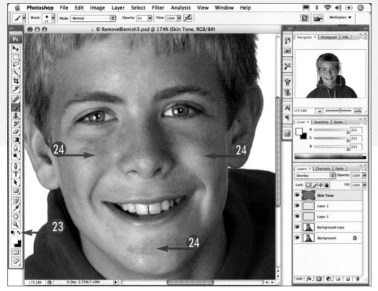

23 Click here to reverse the colors, making white the foreground color.

24 Paint over any dark spots in the image to smooth the skin.

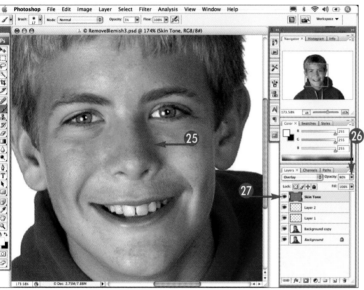

The skin tone appears smoother.

25 Continue painting over any dark areas, adjusting the size of the brush tool as necessary.

26 Click here and drag the Layer Opacity slider to the left to reduce the effect for a more natural look.

27 Click the Visibility icon for the gray layer off and on to compare the image before and after the adjustment.

The skin tone is smoothed and appears natural rather than over-corrected.

TIPS

More Options!

You can press the X key to reverse the background and foreground colors and paint with black to darken any areas that appear too light. However, if your image starts to appear unnatural, open the History palette and click back several steps to undo the changes. Then continue painting until the skin tone appears natural.

Attention!

You may not see much of a change as you paint with the Brush opacity set to 3%; however, when you turn off the Visibility icon for the layer, you will definitely see the changes. You can increase or decrease the brush opacity one or two percent, brush over an area, and then check the changes by toggling on and off the Visibility icon.

REMOVE RED EYE
to quickly improve any photo

You can remove the red-eye effect from all photographs, whether they are scanned from film or prints or start out as digital files. Photoshop CS3 includes a Red Eye tool that makes the process very easy.

Red eye is caused by the reflection of a camera flash in a person's retina. When you shoot in a darkened room, the subject's irises are wide open and their pupils enlarged, increasing the chances for red-eye photos. Using a camera with the flash mounted

directly above the lens also causes more red eyes than using a bounce flash or a flash unit that is positioned away from the camera lens.

By default, Photoshop's Red Eye tool uses a large brush and makes the areas around the pupil black. You can change the default settings in the Options bar to fit the size of your subject's eyes. Changing the red areas to a dark gray color rather than black makes your subject look more natural and enables you to change the eye color later if needed.

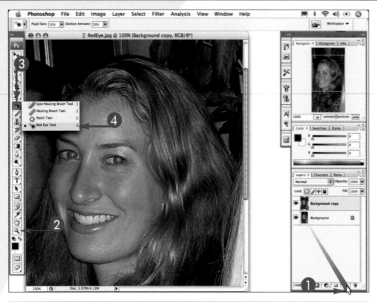

1 With the image open, drag the Background layer over the New Layer icon to duplicate it.

2 Click the Zoom tool and zoom in to enlarge the red eyes.

3 Click and hold the Spot Healing Brush tool to reveal its other tool options.

4 Click the Red Eye tool.

The Options bar changes to show the options for the Red Eye tool.

5 Double-click here and type **15**.

6 Make sure that the Darken Amount data field is set to 50.

7 Click in the red area of one eye.

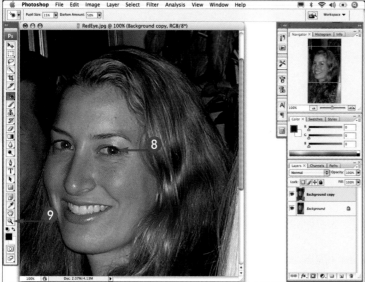

Photoshop replaces the red with a neutral gray.

⑧ Click in the red area of the other eye.

Photoshop again replaces the red with a neutral gray.

⑨ Click the Zoom tool.

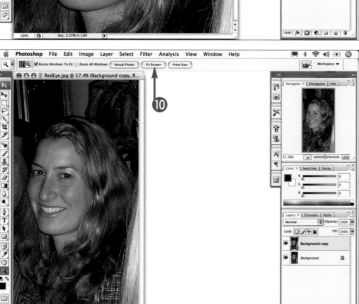

The Options bar changes.

⑩ Click Fit Screen.

Photoshop zooms out, so you can see the entire image and the more natural-looking eye color.

TIPS

Did You Know?

Pressing J selects the Spot Healing Brush tool. Press Shift as you press J again three times to select the Red Eye tool. With the tool selected, press Return (Enter), and the first data field in the Options bar is highlighted. Type your settings and press Tab to highlight the next data field.

Try This!

You can select all the tools even faster using a one-letter keyboard shortcut. Click Photoshop (Edit) → Preferences → General. Deselect the Use Shift Key for Tool Switch check box in the Options section of the dialog box. Click OK. When you press the letter corresponding to a tool, you cycle through all the tools hidden below the first one.

CHANGE EYE COLOR
digitally

Using the Red Eye tool works well to eliminate the red-eye effect. However, it leaves the eyes a black or gray color. You can improve many photos by simply adding back a little color or colorizing the iris of the eyes.

When you colorize the eyes, you are looking for a natural eye color. If you have another photo of the same person, you can sample the eye color from the first photo and paint it into the one with gray eyes. You can also select any color as the foreground color

and paint in the irises. Colorizing the eyes naturally depends on specific brush options you set in the Options bar.

You can also use the same technique to apply one person's eye color to another subject's eyes. Agencies often request a specific eye color for a model to better blend into the color scheme of an advertising piece. You can save time by using Photoshop to change the eye color in the original photo and avoid finding and photographing a different model.

Photo © 2007 www.photospin.com

① Click and drag the Background layer over the New Layer icon to duplicate the layer as a safety step.

② Click the Zoom tool and zoom in to enlarge the eyes.

③ Click the Eyedropper tool.

④ Click here and select 3 by 3 Average.

⑤ Click in the iris to set a reference color as the foreground color.

⑥ Click the Brush tool.

The Options bar changes.

⑦ Click here to open the Brush Picker.

⑧ Drag the Master Diameter slider to set a brush size just smaller than one-half the iris.

⑨ Click and drag the Hardness slider to 50 percent.

⑩ Click the Airbrush button to enable it.

⑪ Click the Foreground Color box in the toolbox.

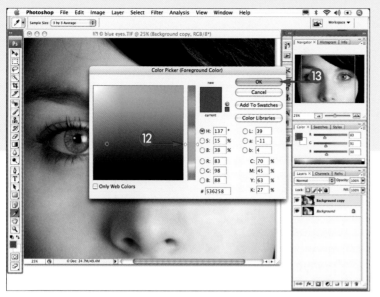

The Color Picker dialog box appears.

12 Click and drag the Hue slider to another color.

13 Click OK to close the Color Picker.

14 Click here to add a new empty layer.

15 Click here and select Color for the layer blend mode.

16 Click and drag over both irises to paint in the new color.

17 Click the Eraser tool and erase if you paint over other areas.

18 Click here and drag the slider to the left until the eye color appears natural.

The eyes now appear the new color.

TIPS

More Options!

If you have another photo with an appropriate eye color, you can also use the Color Replacement tool instead of the standard Brush tool. Select that tool. Press Option+click in the first photo to sample the color of the eyes that you want to use. Then apply the color with soft brush strokes on the empty layer of the image you are correcting.

Did You Know?

You can avoid red eye in many photos if you use the red-eye reduction feature included with some newer cameras. This feature minimizes the red-eye effect in flash photos by firing several flashes an instant before the photo is taken, forcing the pupils to close slightly just as the final flash and shutter are released.

REDUCE WRINKLES
with a soft touch

You can remove wrinkles with Photoshop in a variety of ways, including cloning them away with the Clone Stamp tool or patching them using the Patch tool. However, if you remove all the wrinkles and give a person perfectly smooth skin, the effect is not believable. Using the Healing Brush tool and a separate layer, you can maintain more control over the corrections and give your subject a rejuvenated yet natural appearance.

You can modify the Healing Brush and change its shape and angle so that your brush strokes are not

as visible when you literally paint away the wrinkles. You can create your wrinkle-removing brush by changing attributes in the Brush Picker in the Options bar. The effect appears even more realistic if you use a pressure-sensitive pen tablet and set the Healing Brush to respond to pressure.

After you brush away the years, you can change the opacity of the altered layer to reintroduce just enough wrinkles to appear natural.

Photo © 2007 www.photospin.com

① Click and drag the Background layer thumbnail over the New Layer icon to duplicate the layer.

② Click the Zoom tool and zoom in to enlarge the areas with wrinkles.

③ Click here to add a new empty layer.

④ Click and hold the Spot Healing Brush tool and select the Healing Brush.

⑤ Click here to open the Brush Picker.

⑥ Set the Master Diameter slider to a brush size wide enough to cover the deepest wrinkles.

⑦ Drag the Hardness slider to about 50 percent.

⑧ Click one dot on the circle in the thumbnail and drag toward the center to change the roundness of the brush.

⑨ Drag the arrowhead to change the angle of the stroke in the direction of the deepest wrinkles.

⑩ Click here and select All Layers.

⑪ Press Option+click (Alt+click) an area of clear skin near one wrinkle to sample.

⑫ Click and drag directly on the first wrinkles to paint them away.

⑬ Click here and repeat steps **8** to **12**, changing the brush angle and roundness for the other wrinkles.

⑭ Click the Zoom tool.

⑮ Press Option (Alt) and click in the image to zoom out.

#34

DIFFICULTY LEVEL

⑯ With the top layer selected, click here and drag the slider until the wrinkles appear diminished and still natural.

The wrinkles on the face are less pronounced, and the person appears slightly rested and younger.

TIPS

Try This!
Use many small strokes rather than one larger one when you paint over wrinkles with the Healing Brush and sample nearby areas of clear skin often. The skin tones match more closely, and the results appear more natural.

Try This!
You need to zoom in and out often when removing wrinkles. Instead of changing tools when the Healing Brush is selected, press ⌘+spacebar (Ctrl+spacebar) and click to zoom in. Press Option+ spacebar (Alt+spacebar) to zoom out.

Customize It!
With a Wacom Intuos3 pen, you can set the rocker switch on the pen to the Option (Alt) key. You can then press the rocker switch instead of reaching for your keyboard to sample areas with the Healing Brush tool.

WHITEN TEETH
to improve a smile

You can greatly improve every portrait in which the subject is smiling by applying a little digital tooth whitening. Yellow teeth always dull a smile as well as the overall look of the photo.

You first select the teeth and soften the selection, to avoid a visible line between the areas that are lightened and the rest of the image. Although there are many ways to make a selection in Photoshop, using the Quick Mask mode or the Quick Selection tool as described in Chapter 2 works well when making a detailed selection such as selecting a person's teeth.

After the teeth are selected, whitening is a two-step process. You have to remove the yellow and then brighten the teeth by adjusting the saturation. As in the previous tasks, duplicate the Background layer as a safety step and zoom in to make the detailed selection. Then zoom out to see the whole image before adjusting the color. Digital tooth whitening should be a subtle adjustment to keep the smile and the person looking natural.

① Zoom in and make a selection of the teeth using the Quick Mask mode or the Quick Selection tool.

Note: To use the Quick Mask mode, see Task #17. To use the Quick Selection tool, see Task #16.

② Click Select → Modify → Feather.

The Feather Selection dialog box appears.

③ Type **1** in the Feather Radius field.

④ Click OK.

⑤ Click the Zoom tool and zoom out to see the whole image.

⑥ Press ⌘+H (Ctrl+H) to hide the selection marquee.

The selection marquee is no longer visible, but the teeth are still selected.

⑦ Click Image.

⑧ Click Adjustments.

⑨ Click Hue/Saturation.

The Hue/Saturation dialog box appears.

● If necessary, move the dialog box to one side so that you can see the teeth.

⑩ Click here and select Yellows.

⑪ Click and drag the Saturation slider slowly to the left to remove the yellow.

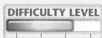
DIFFICULTY LEVEL

⑫ Click here again and select Master.

⑬ Click and drag the Lightness slider slowly to the right to brighten the teeth.

⑭ Click OK to apply the changes.

⑮ Press ⌘+D (Ctrl+D) to deselect the teeth.

TIPS

Try This!
When zooming in on an image, hold the spacebar; the pointer temporarily changes to the Hand tool. You can click and drag around your image with the Hand tool and easily move to the area that needs to be adjusted. When you release the spacebar, you change back to the tool that was previously selected.

Did You Know?
Feathering softens the edge of a selection and smoothes the transition between two distinct areas. You can also click Select → Refine Edge to feather the selection edge. The default settings of the Refine Edge dialog box include a one-pixel feather. Click OK in the dialog box and continue lightening the teeth as shown here.

BRIGHTEN THE EYES
by lightening the whites

One way to quickly enhance a portrait is to draw attention to the eyes. The eyes are the most important feature of the face and the key to a person's individuality. Whether the whites of the eyes are bloodshot or just appear dull, lightening them can enhance the whole face. Brightening and desaturating the white area draws the viewer right into the subject's personality.

Lightening the whites of the eyes is a multistep and multilayer process. You first select the whites and remove the redness using a Hue/Saturation

adjustment layer. Then you brighten the eyes with a Curves adjustment layer and change the blending mode of the layers.

People do not have perfectly white eyes, so this adjustment requires not only making a precise selection, but also viewing the entire photo as you apply the changes. Because the adjustments are on separate layers, you can easily go back and modify the adjustments to enhance the overall image and keep the subject looking natural.

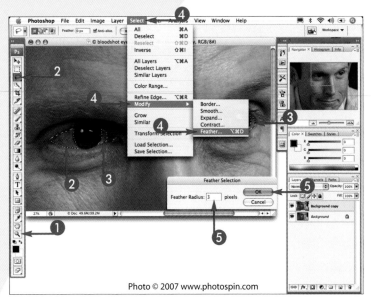

Photo © 2007 www.photospin.com

① With the Background layer duplicated, click the Zoom tool and zoom in on the eye area.

② Click the Lasso tool and draw a selection around the white area of one eye.

③ Press and hold Shift and select the other white areas of the eyes.

④ Click Select ➔ Modify ➔ Feather.

⑤ Type **3** here and click OK.

Note: *A feather radius between 1 and 5 pixels works best for this selection.*

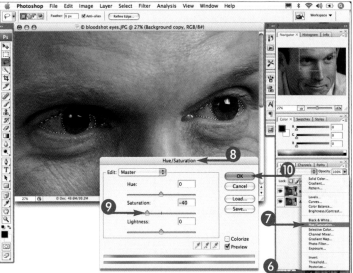

⑥ Click the Adjustment Layer button.

⑦ Click Hue/Saturation.

The Hue/Saturation dialog box appears.

⑧ Move the dialog box so that you can see the eyes.

⑨ Drag the Saturation slider to the left to remove the redness.

⑩ Click OK.

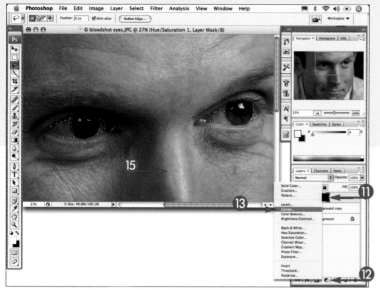

① Press ⌘+click (Ctrl+click) the layer mask thumbnail to load the selection again.

② Click the Adjustment Layer button.

③ Click Curves.

④ Click OK in the Curves dialog box that appears without making any changes.

⑤ Press Option+spacebar (Alt+spacebar) and click in the image to zoom out and see the whole face.

⑥ Click here and select Screen.

⑦ Click here and drag the slider to the left to reduce the opacity of the layer until the eyes look brighter but still natural.

The subject's eyes appear bright without appearing artificially lightened.

36

DIFFICULTY LEVEL

TIPS

More Options!

In some palettes, dialog boxes, and Options bars, clicking and dragging on the word associated with a slider activates the Scrubby sliders. The cursor changes to a pointing finger. Click and drag across the word, changing the amount in the data field.

Did You Know?

Pressing Shift as you select with a selection tool enables you to add to a selected area or add a separate selection. Pressing Option (Alt) as you drag over a selected area enables you to remove areas from that selection.

Try This!

You can quickly access the Feather dialog box, or other options, for any selection by pressing the Ctrl key and clicking (right-clicking) in the selection area. A pop-up contextual menu appears listing options such as Feather and Select Inverse.

ADD DEPTH TO EYES
to emphasize them

Removing red eye and lightening the whites of the eyes improves any portrait photograph. You can also make your subject more interesting by adding other adjustments that emphasize the eyes. You can add more contrast to the *iris,* the colored portion surrounding the pupil, by lightening some areas and darkening others. You can add depth to the eyes by darkening the eyelashes and the natural outline of the eyes. This digital technique is similar to dodging and burning in the darkroom.

Instead of using Photoshop's Dodge and Burn tools on the image, you can use the Brush tool on

separate blank layers and vary the opacity of each layer to control the adjustments. Painting with white lightens areas. Painting with black darkens areas, lengthens the eyelashes, and adds definition to the eyes. Using the Opacity setting in the Layers palette, you can fine-tune the adjustments before you finalize the image.

Making the eyes sparkle by using a variation of digital dodging and burning in Photoshop helps draw the viewer's attention to the eyes and engages them in the photo.

Photo © 2007 www.photospin.com

❶ Click and drag the Background layer over the New Layer button to duplicate it.

❷ Click the New Layer button.

● A new blank layer is added to the Layers palette.

❸ Double-click in the Opacity data field and type **10**.

❹ Click the Zoom tool and click and drag across both eyes to zoom in.

❺ Click here to reset the foreground and background colors to the defaults.

❻ Click here to reverse the foreground and background colors and set the foreground to white.

❼ Click the Brush tool.

8 Click here to open the Brush Picker.

9 Click and drag the Master Diameter slider to select a small brush that fits inside the iris.

10 Click and drag the Hardness slider to 0%.

11 Paint in the center of each iris.

12 Click here to reverse the foreground and background colors and set the foreground to black.

13 Paint with black around the edges of the irises and in the pupils.

14 Click the New Layer button to add a second blank layer.

15 Double-click in the Opacity data field and type **20**.

16 Click the Brushes button to open the Brushes palette and presets.

17 Press ⌘+spacebar (Ctrl+spacebar) and then click in the image to zoom in to see the eyelashes.

TIPS

Did You Know?

You can save and reuse an eyelash brush. With the settings that you create for Brush Tip Shape, click the palette menu arrow on the right in the Brushes palette. Click New Brush Preset. Type a name in the dialog box and click OK.

Try This!

Press D to set the foreground and background colors to the default black and white. Press X to quickly switch the foreground and background colors as you digitally dodge and burn.

Try This!

To lighten dark brown eyes, try setting the foreground color to a dark red or burgundy color instead of white. Paint in the irises on a separate layer and adjust the opacity. Adding red to dark brown eyes softens the look.

ADD DEPTH TO EYES
to emphasize them

Retouching portraits is always tricky. You want to improve the image and still preserve the person's character. Because the eyes can define personality, enhancing the eyes almost always helps the overall portrait and helps the viewer focus on the subject.

When you work on any portrait and especially when you work on the eyes, you need to make small changes. Large changes are too often obvious, and your subjects want to see themselves and be seen at their best, not different. Make small changes and repeat these on several layers. You can easily adjust

the opacity of each layer independently, creating more variations in brush strokes and colors. With adjustments on multiple layers, it is also easier to change or delete enhancements that do not seem natural.

Using a pressure-sensitive pen tablet also gives more variety to brush strokes. Use light brush strokes instead of heavy ones. Many of the brush options can be set to respond to pressure or tilt, allowing you to alter brush styles with fewer trips to the Brushes palette.

Photo © 2007 www.photospin.com

18 Click Brush Tip Shape.

19 Select a very small brush to match the size of the eyelashes.

20 Drag the dots on the roundness icon and the brush angle to conform the brush shape to the eyelashes of one eye.

21 Click here to close the Brushes palette.

22 Paint over the eyelashes one at a time to darken them.

23 Press the spacebar and click in the image to move to the other eye.

24 Click here and repeat steps **18** to **22**, adjusting the brush to fit the shape of the lashes of the other eye.

25 Press Option+spacebar (Alt+spacebar) and click in the image to zoom out and see the whole face.

26 Click Layer 1 to highlight it.

27 Click in the Opacity data field.

28 Press the keyboard up or down arrows to increase or decrease the opacity until the irises look natural.

#37 CONTINUED

29 Click Layer 2 to highlight it.

30 Click in the Opacity data field.

31 Press the keyboard up or down arrows to increase or decrease the opacity until the eyelashes look darker but still natural.

The eyes now appear stronger and still natural and help focus the viewer's eyes.

TIPS

More Options!

You can add eyeliner to the eyes in a photograph. First add another layer. Lower the opacity to about 18 percent. Paint with black at the edge of the eyelashes on each eye. Click in the Opacity data field and use the keyboard up and down arrows to increase or reduce the opacity of the layer until the eyeliner looks natural.

Did You Know?

You can use the same technique shown in this task to enhance light eyebrows. Add a layer and reduce the opacity to 8 percent. Open the Brushes palette and click Brush Tip Shape. Set the hardness to 0 percent and change the size, angle, and roundness to match the shape of the eyebrows. Paint a few smooth strokes over both eyebrows using black. Change the layer's opacity as needed.

ADD A CATCH LIGHT
to make the eyes come alive

When the light source — whether it comes from a camera flash, side lighting, or a natural light source — reflects in the subject's eyes, it forms a catch light. A catch light, or a specular highlight, in a subject's eyes adds life and sparkle to the subject and brightens the overall photograph. More importantly, it draws attention to the subject's eyes and engages the viewer.

If the subject in a photograph does not have any specular highlights in the eyes or if the subject's eyes appear somewhat dull, you can use Photoshop to add catch lights.

Jane Conner-ziser, one of the most experienced and well-respected portrait retouching masters, teaches this technique in her classes and instructional videos. Jane creates catch lights with diffused edges and emphasizes the use of two separate layers, one for the glow and the other for the sparkle of catch lights. By placing them on separate layers, you can adjust the catch lights to achieve a natural look.

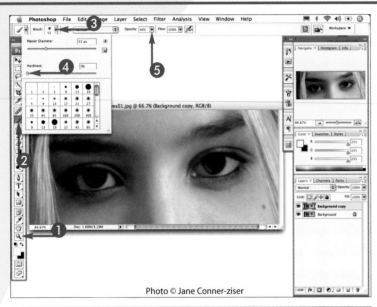

Photo © Jane Conner-ziser

① With the Background layer duplicated, click the Zoom tool and zoom in on the eye area.

② Click the Brush tool.

③ Click here and select a brush slightly larger than the final catch light should be.

④ Click and drag the hardness slider to 0%.

⑤ Click here and drag the slider to 40%.

⑥ Press D to reset the foreground and background colors.

⑦ Press X to reverse the colors, making white the foreground color.

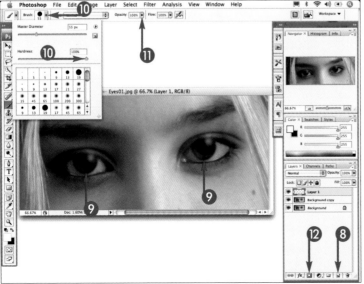

⑧ Click here to add a new empty layer.

⑨ Click once in each eye to create the catch lights.

⑩ Click here and drag the Hardness slider completely to the right (100%).

⑪ Click here and drag the slider to the right to return the brush opacity to 100%.

⑫ Click here to add a layer mask.

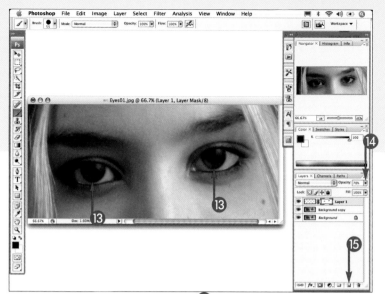

The foreground color changes to black.

⑬ Paint over the top of the catch light so that it conforms to the upper eyelid.

⑭ Click here and drag the layer opacity to 70%.

⑮ Click the New Layer button to make a new empty layer.

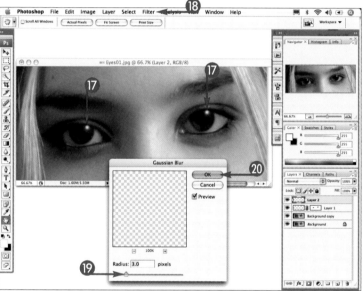

The foreground color changes to white.

⑯ Press the [key multiple times to reduce the brush size to about half the previous size.

⑰ Click once in the center of each catch light.

⑱ Click Filter → Blur → Gaussian Blur.

The Gaussian Blur dialog box appears.

⑲ Click and drag the Radius slider between 1.5 and 3 pixels to soften the edges.

⑳ Click OK.

A soft-edged catch light with a sparkle in the center appears in each eye.

TIPS

More Options!

Zoom out to see the whole face. Click and drag the Layer Opacity slider for each of the catch light layers until you see a bright sparkle with a natural diffused edge.

Attention!

The catch lights must correspond to the natural direction of the light to appear natural. If the light is coming from the right, the catch lights should be on the right side of the pupils, just slightly above the center.

Did You Know?

Jane Conner-ziser is not only one of the best-known photo retouchers in the industry, but she is also a Corel Painter master. She teaches portrait photography, photo retouching, and fine art at venues throughout the world, as well as at her School of Digital Arts in Florida.

SHARPEN JUST THE EYES
to add focus

The final step to enhancing the eyes in a photograph is to sharpen the eye area. You want to add focus and draw the viewer into the photo, but you may not want to sharpen the rest of the face or the skin. You can selectively sharpen the eyes by using a Sharpen filter and then applying the filter with the History palette and History Brush.

The techniques for sharpening in Photoshop had not really changed until the release of Photoshop CS2. As with that previous version, you can use not only

the Unsharp Mask filter for sharpening, but also the new Smart Sharpen filter. This filter is not only easier to use, but it also has added features including a much larger preview.

After you sharpen the entire portrait, you can hide the effect using the History palette to go back to a version of the photo before the sharpening was applied. Then using the History Brush, you can paint the sharpening effect on the eye area where you want the focus.

Photo © 2007 www.photospin.com

① Click and drag the Background layer over the New Layer button to duplicate it.

② Double-click the Zoom tool to view the image at 100 percent.

③ Press the spacebar, click in the image, and move it to see the eyes.

④ Click Filter.

⑤ Click Sharpen.

⑥ Click Smart Sharpen.

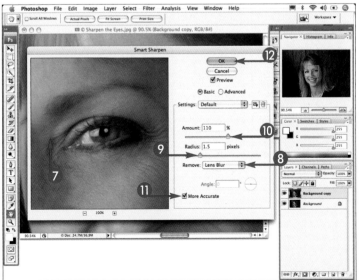

The Smart Sharpen dialog box appears.

⑦ Click in the Preview window and drag to see the eyes area.

⑧ Click here and select Lens Blur.

⑨ Click and drag the Radius slider to 1.5.

⑩ Click and drag the Amount slider to sharpen the eye, generally between 80 and 115 percent.

⑪ Click More Accurate.

⑫ Click OK to apply the sharpening.

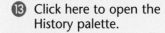

The Smart Sharpen
filter progress bar
appears, and sharpening
is applied to the
Background copy layer.

⑬ Click here to open the
History palette.

⑭ Click the box to the left
of the Smart Sharpen step
to set the source for the
History Brush.

⑮ Click the previous state in
the History palette.

⑯ Click here to close the
History palette.

⑰ Click the History Brush tool.

⑱ Click here to open the Brush Picker.

⑲ Select a soft-edge brush at 0 percent
Hardness that is large enough to cover the
edge of the eyes.

⑳ Paint over the eyes, eyelashes, and
eyebrows with the History Brush to apply
the sharpening.

㉑ Click the Visibility icon for the Background
copy on and off to compare before and
after sharpening.

The sharpening is applied only to the eye
areas.

#39

DIFFICULTY LEVEL

Attention!

The Smart Sharpen filter only applies
to one layer. If you have made other
adjustment layers, you must merge them
before applying the sharpening. Press
⌘+Option+Shift+E (Ctrl+Alt+Shift+E).
The adjustment layers and the
Background layers merge in the
new layer. All the adjustment layers,
Background copy, and original
Background layers remain unchanged.

Did You Know?

Always view the image at 100%
magnification when you use a
sharpening filter to get the most accurate
view onscreen of your changes. Still, the
amount of detail visible in a print may be
slightly different than what you see on
the screen. The amount of detail can vary
depending on the type of printer and
paper used.

ADD A SOFT-FOCUS EFFECT
to make a portrait glow

You can apply Photoshop's filters to mimic the photographic filters used in traditional film photography. However, by using a combination of Photoshop filters, layers, and blending modes, you can add special effects and create unique images with a painterly quality that go beyond the possibilities of film photography. You can add a soft-focus effect to a portrait that not only minimizes skin imperfections but also adds a romantic glow to the subject's skin and still keeps the subject's main features in focus.

You first apply a filter and change the blending mode to modify the effect. Make other changes using the

layer's opacity setting. When the overall effect is pleasing, you can refocus the eyes and other areas to help draw the viewer into the portrait.

Whenever you use various filters, you can control the effects by working on a duplicate of the original Background layer and then adjust the effects with layer modes and opacity changes. Duplicated layers are also great for experimenting with different creative techniques. If you do not like the changes, simply delete the layer.

Photo © 2007 www.photospin.com

① Click and drag the Background layer over the New Layer button to duplicate it.

② Click Filter.

③ Click Convert for Smart Filters.

④ Click OK in the message box.

The Background copy layer is changed into a smart object.

⑤ Click Filter.

⑥ Click Blur.

⑦ Click Gaussian Blur.

● When the Gaussian Blur dialog box appears, move it to the side to see the photo.

⑧ Click and drag the Radius slider to blur the image.

Note: Use a blur of 4 to 8 pixels for low resolution and 10 to 14 pixels for high-resolution images.

⑨ Click OK to apply the blur.

⑩ Click here and select Screen.

The image becomes very light.

⑪ Click here to add a layer mask.

The foreground color is set to black.

⑫ Press B to select the Brush tool.

⑬ Click here to open the Brush Picker.

⑭ Click a soft-edged brush just large enough to outline the eye area.

⑮ Click the Airbrush thumbnail.

⑯ Click here and drag the slider to the left until 40% appears in the Opacity field.

⑰ Paint over the eyes and other important features to bring them out.

⑱ Click here and drag the Layer Opacity slider to the left to get the amount of glow that you want.

The soft focus is applied to the overall portrait while keeping the main features of the subject in sharp focus.

40

Did You Know?

Dragging the Background layer over the New Layer button automatically names the duplicated layer "Background copy." You can also duplicate the Background layer by pressing ⌘+J (Ctrl+J). This duplicated Background layer is named "Layer 1."

Try This!

To experiment with the amount of Gaussian Blur, or any other smart filter, double-click the filter name in the Layers palette to reopen the dialog box. Change the slider amounts and watch the changes on your image.

More Options!

You can select and modify brushes from either the Brush Picker in the Options bar or from the floating Brushes palette. When you edit or save a brush in one place, the brush is automatically updated in the other.

Chapter 5

Changing and Enhancing Colors and Tone

Color is the heart of Photoshop. Whether you work on a design or a photograph, you often adjust the hue, saturation, and brightness of an image. Using Photoshop, you can fine-tune shadows and highlights or completely alter the overall tone of a photograph. You can transform a color photograph into a grayscale image, colorize an old grayscale image, or make a color image look like an antique colorized photograph. You can also tone a photo as photographers used to do in the darkroom. And you can create these effects in many different ways.

Because some pixel information is discarded whenever you make color and tonal adjustments, you should apply corrections on separate layers or on a duplicate layer. Photoshop CS3's adjustment layers help you make some changes without permanently altering pixel values. In addition, opening or converting an image or a layer to a new smart object enables you to apply most filters as smart filters, making them continuously editable and nondestructive. You can reedit adjustment layers and smart filters before you flatten the image.

Camera Raw 4, included with Photoshop CS3, not only adds powerful controls for editing images, but it can also open a variety of file formats, including JPEGs and TIFFs, so you can start with nondestructive edits in Camera Raw for most photos.

Whenever you make color or tonal adjustments, start by calibrating and profiling your monitor. Otherwise, you may be changing colors that are not really in the image, and what you see on your monitor can look very different when it is printed.

Top 100

IMPROVE AN UNDEREXPOSED PHOTO
in two steps

You may find a photograph that is perfect for your project or has the subject just the way you want, but it is underexposed. Fixing an underexposed photograph with traditional photography tools was difficult. Fixing such a photo with Photoshop is much easier, and there are many ways you can accomplish the correction. You can use a variety of Photoshop filters and adjustments to correct the exposure. However, you can sometimes easily make a quick correction using a duplicated layer and altering the layer blend mode. This two-step technique is worth

a try before you work with any of the other methods.

Depending on the photo, the exposure may appear corrected the first time that you apply the technique. For other images, you may need to repeat the steps once or even twice. You can even apply a half step by duplicating the layer with the changed blend mode and reducing the effect by changing the opacity of the layer. You can also adjust the Fill slider to lower the effect of the layer without altering any layer styles on that layer.

① With an underexposed photo open in Photoshop, click and drag the Background layer over the New Layer button to duplicate it.

② Click here and select Screen.

The photo appears lighter.

Note: The photo may look fine this way, or you may need to add another layer and change it as in steps 3 to 4.

③ Click and drag the Background copy layer over the New Layer button to duplicate the copy.

④ Click here and drag the Opacity slider to the left to change the opacity of the top layer and the amount of lightening.

The underexposed image exposure is improved.

IMPROVE AN OVEREXPOSED PHOTO
in three steps

An overexposed photograph is impossible to salvage with traditional darkroom techniques. Too much light means that there is nothing in the film to print. Digital photography and Photoshop can change and improve photos in new and almost magical ways. Although it may be easier to lighten a dark photo, you can easily reduce some of the highlights in an overly bright photograph and often improve the image enough to make it worth printing. You can use the Shadow/Highlight command in the basic mode to effectively reduce the highlights.

With most dialog boxes in Photoshop, when you move the slider to the right you increase the amount. When you use the Shadow/Highlight adjustment to reduce the highlights, it works in the opposite fashion.

As with every project in Photoshop, you can accomplish the task in a variety of ways. This three-step technique for reducing the highlights and improving an overexposed photo is so easy that it is always worth testing before spending time with other methods or discarding the photo.

① Click and drag the Background layer over the New Layer button to duplicate it.

② Click Filter.

③ Click Convert for Smart Filters.

● The Background copy layer is converted to a smart object.

④ Click Image.

⑤ Click Adjustments.

⑥ Click Shadow/Highlight.

● When the Shadow/Highlights dialog box appears, move the dialog box so that you can see the image.

⑦ Click and drag this slider to 0.

⑧ Click and drag this slider to the right until the image looks the way you want.

● Optionally, you can click Show More Options to refine the adjustment.

⑨ Click OK.

The image exposure is improved.

REMOVE A COLORCAST
to improve the overall color

Whether you have a scanned image or one from a digital camera, your image may show a colorcast due to improper lighting, white balance settings, or other factors. A *colorcast* appears as a reddish, bluish, or greenish tint over the whole image. Photoshop has many tools that you can use to remove colorcasts, including the White Balance setting in Camera Raw, and sometimes you may need to try different ones, depending on the photograph. Using the Match Color command as shown here to remove a colorcast is simple and often works well.

Intended for matching the colors between two images, the Match Color command uses advanced algorithms to adjust the brightness, color saturation, and color balance in an image. Because you can adjust the controls in different combinations, using this command on just one image gives you better control over the color and luminance of the image than many other tools.

When using the Match Color command on a duplicated layer, you can use the layer's Opacity slider to fade the effect to achieve the best color for your image, as well as compare the before and after images.

❶ Click and drag the Background layer over the New Layer button to duplicate it.

❷ Click Image.

❸ Click Adjustments.

❹ Click Match Color.

● When the Match Color dialog box appears, move it to the side so that you can see your image.

❺ Click Neutralize to remove the colorcast.

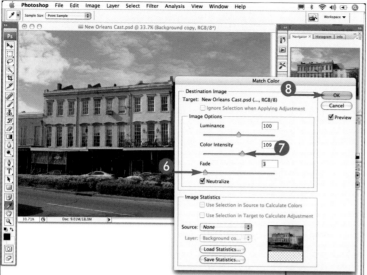

6 Click and drag the Fade slider slowly to the right to reduce the effect, if necessary.

7 Click and drag the Color Intensity slider to the right to increase the color range if necessary.

8 Click OK to apply the change.

43
DIFFICULTY LEVEL

9 Click here and drag the slider to adjust the overall effect if necessary.

The colorcast is removed, and the colors appear more natural.

TIPS

Did You Know?

You can view the floating Histogram palette and see the color changes as they are made. Click the palette menu on the Histogram tab and click All Channels View. Click the palette menu again and click Show Channels in Color. Click and drag the Histogram palette so that you can keep it open and still see the image and your other palettes.

More Options!

If there is an area in the image that is normally neutral gray, you can also correct a colorcast using the Levels command. Click Layer → New Adjustment Layer → Levels. Click OK in the New Layer dialog box. Click the Gray Point eyedropper, the middle eyedropper in the Levels dialog box. Click in the part of the image that should be neutral gray.

COLORIZE
an old black-and-white photograph

Hand-coloring a photograph can be a difficult process using traditional paints and traditional film photos. With Photoshop, hand-coloring an old black-and-white image is much easier. You can use any black-and-white photo, called a *grayscale image,* and paint areas using any colors that you choose.

You can start with larger areas and then focus in on specific parts to colorize individually and on additional layers. By making selections of detailed areas and then applying the colors, you can be as

precise as necessary to achieve the effect. Zoom in to select and paint detailed areas and then zoom out to see the overall effect. Continue making different selections and choosing other colors until the whole image is colorized.

You can vary the size of the Brush tool as you paint or use a pressure-sensitive stylus and set the brush size to Pressure. After the entire image is painted, you can lower the opacity of each colored layer as a final touch.

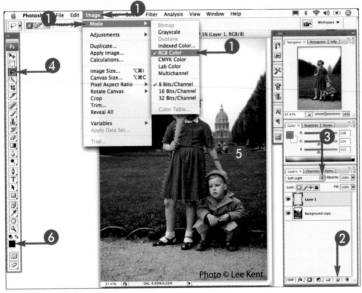

① Click Image → Mode → RGB Color.

The color mode changes, but the image on the screen does not.

② Click the New Layer button in the Layers palette.

③ Click here and select Soft Light.

④ Click the Lasso tool.

⑤ Click and draw around an area to make a selection.

⑥ Click in the foreground color in the toolbox.

The Color Picker dialog box appears.

⑦ Click and drag the Color slider to select a color range.

⑧ Click in the Color Preview box to select a color.

⑨ Click OK to close the dialog box.

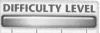

⑩ Press B to select the Brush tool.

⑪ Click here to open the Brush Picker.

⑫ Click a soft-edged brush.

⑬ Paint over the selected areas to apply the color.

DIFFICULTY LEVEL

⑭ Click here and drag the Opacity slider for the layer to adjust the color.

⑮ Repeat steps **2** to **14** until the entire image is painted.

The black-and-white photo now appears in color.

TIPS

Try This!

Instead of clicking the foreground color, simply click in the Set Foreground Color box in the Color palette to open the Color Picker without changing tools. You can also move the cursor over the Color palette and click in the multicolored bar to select a color — all without changing tools. Click and drag the RGB sliders to adjust the colors.

More Options!

You can select more realistic colors for skin tones or hair by selecting the colors from another color image. Keep the other image open on the screen while you are colorizing the grayscale photo. With the Color Picker open, move the cursor outside the dialog box to sample real colors from the color image. Then paint in the grayscale image with those colors.

Make a
QUICK CHANGE TO GRAYSCALE

You can convert a color image to grayscale in many ways in Photoshop. You want to preserve as much of the image data as possible to be able to vary the range of tones. Changing the mode of the file to grayscale discards pixel data and gives you an image that appears flat and has a small tonal range. Selecting Desaturate from the Image Adjustments menu also tends to flatten the contrast. You can make a quick change using an adjustment layer instead and never alter any of the original image pixels. Using a Gradient Map, you effectively map the

range of tones in an image to the foreground and background colors. Changing the layer blend mode adjusts the gray tones.

Even if you want the end result to be a black-and-white photograph, shoot the photo in color and scan black-and-white photos in the RGB mode. There is more pixel data in an RGB image than in a grayscale image — almost three times as much. You can always remove the color from a photograph, but you cannot put real colors back in.

Photo © 2007 www.photospin.com

① Click and drag the Background layer over the New Layer button to duplicate it as a safety step.

② Press D to reset the foreground and background colors to the default black and white.

③ Click the New Adjustment Layer button.

④ Click Gradient Map.

The Gradient Map dialog box appears, and the image behind it changes to grayscale.

⑤ Click OK to close the dialog box without making any changes.

⑥ Click here.

⑦ Click Color.

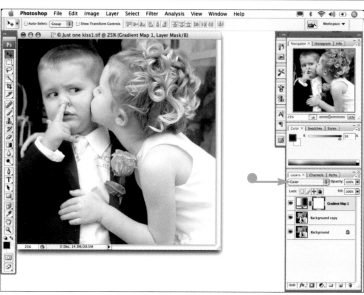

● The Layer blend mode changes to Color, and the values in the image change to show more gradations in the grays.

Optionally, you can press ⌘ (Ctrl)+E to merge the Gradient Map layer with the Background copy layer.

 TIPS

Attention!

The quick grayscale conversion technique shown here works best with correctly exposed photos. Be sure to adjust the exposure before applying the Gradient Map adjustment layer.

Did You Know?

You can turn an image to sepia, or any other color, by clicking the Foreground Color box and selecting a color instead of black. For a sepia tone, try setting the RGB values in the Color Picker to 172, 122, 42. Then follow the steps here to map a sepia-to-white gradient over the image.

More Options!

The various layer blend modes change how a layer interacts with the layer below it. You can cycle through the blend modes using the keyboard. Press V to select the Move tool. Then press Shift++ repeatedly.

Give a new photo an
OLD COLORIZED LOOK

You can hand-color an old grayscale photograph with Photoshop to create an antique look. You can also start with a color image, convert it to grayscale as in Task #45, and then colorize it to get a very different look; this type of colorization is much easier to accomplish. You can colorize the entire photo or just one area for effect. With a copy of the original color photo on a layer beneath the grayscale layer, you can use the Eraser tool with a low Opacity setting and bring the original color back in specific areas. You

can even create a more or less muted colorized effect by changing the opacity of the tool as you erase.

If you have already saved the grayscale photo without the original layers, you can still use the method shown here. First open both the original color image and the converted grayscale photo. Using the Move tool, hold the Shift key as you click and drag the grayscale version onto the original color photo. Then follow steps **5** to **12** below to paint a very creative image.

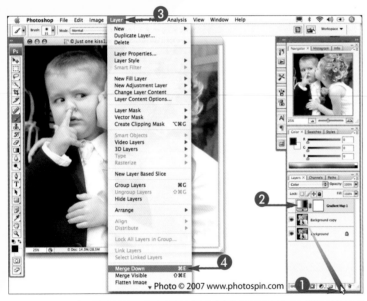

Photo © 2007 www.photospin.com

1 Click and drag the Background layer over the New Layer button to duplicate it.

2 Follow steps **2** to **7** of Task #45 to add the Gradient Map layer.

3 Click Layer.

4 Click Merge Down.

The top two layers merge in the Layers palette, leaving only the Background copy layer in grayscale and the Background layer in color.

5 Click the Eraser tool.

6 Click here and select a brush size.

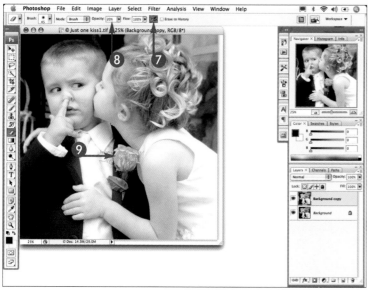

7. Click the Airbrush button.

8. Double-click here and type **20**.

9. Erase over the area to be colorized.

46

DIFFICULTY LEVEL

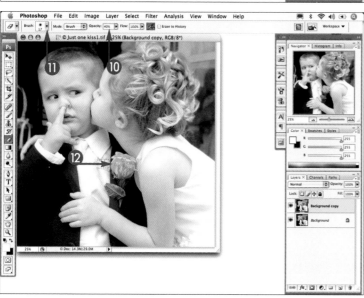

10. Double-click here again and type **40**.

11. Click here and drag the slider to reduce the brush size.

12. Erase over parts of the colored area to increase the color.

The viewer's attention is drawn to the perfect spot.

TIPS

Did You Know?

You can change the size of the Eraser tool by pressing] to increase the size and [to reduce the size. You can also change the opacity of the Eraser tool by clicking once in the Opacity data field and pressing the up arrow on the keyboard for an increase or the down arrow for a decrease.

Did You Know?

You can vary the hardness or softness of the Eraser or Brush tools using the keyboard instead of the Brush Picker. Click the Eraser or Brush tool to select it. Hold the Shift key down as you repeatedly press] to increase the hardness or [to increase the softness.

Using Camera Raw to
RECOVER HIGHLIGHTS

Camera Raw 4, which comes with Photoshop CS3, adds many improvements and new features to the previous edition, making it a powerful image editor on its own. One of the many valuable additions in this new version is the Recovery slider. Clipped highlights, where the image shows no pixel information, are very difficult to adjust and can ruin an otherwise good photograph.

With an image open in Camera Raw, you can see the blown-out highlights by clicking the top right triangle in the histogram. The highlights without any colored pixels appear in red. Conversely, clicking the left triangle in the histogram makes the overly dark shadow areas or completely black areas with no tonal range appear in blue.

The Recovery slider works in combination with the Exposure slider. Using both sliders, you can improve the exposure and prevent most of the highlights from being completely blown out.

The Exposure and the Recovery sliders are located on the Basic tab of the new Camera Raw dialog box.

① Open the Bridge.

② Click a photo to select it.

③ Click File.

④ Click Open in Camera Raw.

Note: You can also open most camera manufacturer's Raw files by double-clicking the file in any folder or in the Bridge.

The photo opens in the Camera Raw dialog box.

⑤ Click here to view the overexposed highlights.

⑥ Click here to view the underexposed shadows.

- White highlights appear in red and black shadows appear in blue.

- Optionally, you can click and drag the Exposure slider to the right slowly to increase the exposure.

⑦ Click and drag the Recovery slider slowly to the right to lessen the red colored areas.

The red colored highlights are reduced.

⑧ Click and drag the Exposure slider slowly to the left to reduce the red colored highlights more.

⑨ Repeat steps **7** and **8** as needed to adjust the photo.

The blown-out highlights are reduced, and the photo displays a better exposure.

 TIPS

Did You Know?
You can click any JPEG or TIFF image in the Bridge and then click File → Open in Camera Raw, or press ⌘+R (Ctrl+R), to open that file in Camera Raw.

Did You Know?
You can also open JPEGs or TIFFs into Camera Raw directly from Photoshop. Click File → Open. Navigate to and select the photo in the Open dialog box. Click the Format arrow and select Camera Raw before clicking Open.

More Options!
The Fill Light slider in Camera Raw 4 performs changes similar to the Shadow/ Highlight adjustment in Photoshop CS3. The Fill Light slider brightens only the shadows without changing other values. The Blacks slider changes the black points in the photo, darkening it.

IMPROVE A SKY
with HSL values in Camera Raw

When you first open an image in Camera Raw 4, the interface displays the numerous color and tone adjustments on the Basic tab. These sliders help you adjust the tone, white balance, and saturation of the overall image. On other tabs, you can adjust different tones and colors individually, make lens corrections, sharpen and reduce noise, and even save some of your settings as presets so that you can reapply them to similar images.

The new HSL/Grayscale tab opens some of the most powerful controls for altering the colors in images.

For example, you can easily dramatize the sky in a landscape photo by changing the luminance values of the blues or other colors and completely change the mood of the image.

The Hue, Saturation, and Luminance sliders on the HSL/Grayscale tab are completely subjective. You control the colors in the image by what you see on the screen, so it is essential to work with a properly calibrated and profiled monitor.

① Open an image with a large sky area in Camera Raw by following steps **1** to **4** in Task #47.

② Click here.

The panel changes to the HSL/Grayscale options and shows the Hue sliders.

● Optionally, you can move the Purples slider to adjust the colors in the sky.

③ Click the Luminance tab.

The panel changes to show the Luminance sliders.

④ Click and drag the Blues slider to the left to deepen the blues in the sky.

DIFFICULTY LEVEL

The color of the sky is dramatically deepened.

● Optionally, you can click and drag the Purples Luminance slider to remove some of the haze.

● You can click Open Image to open the photo in Photoshop.

TIPS

Did You Know?
Each of the three separate sub tabs on the HSL/Grayscale tab — for hue, saturation, and luminance — has the same set of color sliders, yet each color is controlled independently of the others.

Important!
The sub tabs of the HSL/Grayscale tab of Camera Raw 4 have separate default settings. If you want to revert back to the default settings, you must reset each tab separately by clicking on each Default button separately.

Try This!
Use each slider on the Hue sub tab to adjust the individual colors separately. Use the Saturation sub tab to increase or decrease the saturation of a range of specific tones. Use the Luminance sub tab to brighten or darken each color range separately.

Go from color to grayscale with the

NEW BLACK & WHITE ADJUSTMENT

With so many techniques for changing a color image to black and white, and without fixed rules on which colors in an image should match specific levels of gray, you can create a variety of different grayscale images from one color photograph. The Gradient Map technique described in Task #45 effectively maps the existing colors in the photo to a gradient of black to white. The new Black & White adjustment in Photoshop CS3 offers a new conversion method, more powerful and easier to use than the old channel-mixer method and offering more visual

control. You interactively determine which shade of gray is applied to any particular color range in the image. The adjustment dialog box includes a number of presets that you can modify to suit your photograph, or you can create your own preset and save it from within the dialog box.

Although the Black & White adjustment can be used as a simple adjustment, you should apply the command as an adjustment layer for nondestructive editing and to preserve the original image data.

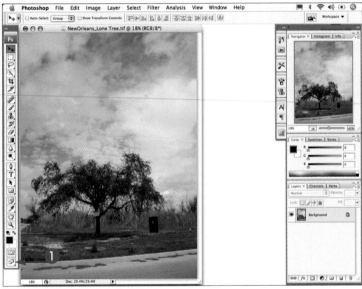

1 With the image that you want to convert to grayscale open in Photoshop, click the Change Screen Mode button two times to view the image against a gray background or three times for a black background.

Note: Changing the screen mode to eliminate distracting colors and other screen elements can help when making visual adjustments to any image.

The background color changes.

2 Press the spacebar and click in the image to center it if necessary.

3 Click here and select Black & White.

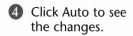

The photo is automatically converted to a grayscale image, and the Black and White dialog box appears.

④ Click Auto to see the changes.

Note: The Auto function in the Black and White dialog box maps different colors to various grays than the default setting.

⑤ Press Option (Alt) and click the Reset button.

Note: The Option (Alt) key changes the Cancel button to Reset.

⑥ Click here and select Infrared.

The grayscale image changes.

⑦ Click in the image and drag to the left on an area you want to darken.

The corresponding slider moves to the left, and the preset changes to Custom.

⑧ Click in the image and drag to the right on an area you want to lighten.

The corresponding slider moves to the right.

● You can click and drag any of the sliders to customize the conversion.

⑨ Click OK to complete the conversion.

TIPS

Change It!
Checking the Tint check box in the Black and White dialog box enables you to color-tone the grayscale image. Drag the Hue slider to the color that you want and then move the Saturation slider to increase the amount of tint.

More Options!
You can also convert a color image in the Camera Raw 4 dialog box by clicking the Convert to Grayscale check box on the HSL/Grayscale tab. Adjust the color sliders to alter the grayscale values corresponding to the colors in the underlying image.

Did You Know?
Although using the Black & White adjustment offers more options for the look of the final grayscale image, the Grayscale conversion in Camera Raw 4 is also quick and nondestructive.

CREATE A SPLIT TONE
for a special effect in Camera Raw

Split-tone effects in the traditional darkroom were difficult and labor intensive. With Camera Raw 4 included with Photoshop CS3, you can easily create a split-tone look, in which a different color is applied to the shadows and highlights. You can also visually add or remove tones while previewing the image.

This new feature of Camera Raw 4 lets you associate hue and saturation to the lightest colors separately from the hue and saturation values to the darkest colors in the image. You can then adjust the Balance slider to emphasize the tone of the highlights or the tone of the shadow areas.

Because you create the split tone in Camera Raw, the alteration to the image is completely nondestructive. The original image always remains intact. You can reopen the Camera Raw dialog box to change the color or saturation amounts any time to adjust the effect.

You can apply a split tone to either a grayscale or a color image; however, the toning is often most effective on a grayscale photo with high contrasts.

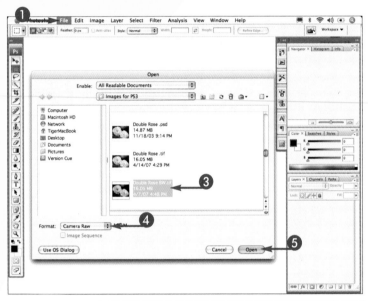

① In Photoshop, click File.

② Click Open.

The Open dialog box appears.

Note: This figure shows the Open dialog box after clicking the Use Adobe Dialog button instead of Use OS Dialog.

③ Navigate to the file and click to select it.

④ Click here and select Camera Raw.

⑤ Click Open.

The Camera Raw dialog box appears.

⑥ Click the Split Toning tab.

7 Click and drag the Highlights Hue slider to select the color for the highlights.

8 Click and drag the Highlights Saturation slider to increase the saturation in the highlight areas.

9 Click and drag the Shadows Hue slider to select the color for the shadows.

10 Click and drag the Shadows Saturation slider to increase the saturation in the shadow areas.

11 Click and drag the Balance slider to the right to shift the toning more into the highlights or to the left to emphasize the tones in the shadows.

12 Repeat steps **7** to **11** to adjust the split-tone effect.

● You can click Open Image to open the toned image and continue editing it in Photoshop or click Save Image to save it with the adjustments and a different name.

The grayscale image appears as a traditional split-tone image with different colored shadows and highlights.

TIPS

Did You Know?
You can automatically open an image in Camera Raw 4 as a smart object. Press Shift and the Open Image button changes to Open Object. Double-clicking the smart object layer in Photoshop reopens the Camera Raw settings.

More Options!
If you add a split tone to a color image, you can still convert it to grayscale after applying split toning. Using the HSB/Grayscale tab, you can also change the effects of the split toning.

Try This!
Leave the Saturation slider set to 0 and press the Option (Alt) key as you drag the Hue sliders. The preview shows a 100 percent saturation of that hue. After you select the hue, move the Saturation sliders to the amount that you want.

Making Magic with Digital Special Effects

Since Photoshop's inception, photographers and graphic designers alike have been using it for digital imaging and photo manipulation. Photoshop can transform an average shot into a good photograph, a good photograph into a great one, and a great image into creative fine art. Photoshop CS3 adds even more power and control to digital image editing. Just as with the previous versions, there are many different ways to create a design or enhance a photograph. You can use the old tools in new ways and in combination with the new techniques to create, improve, or completely alter any image.

You can simulate the effect of using traditional photographic filters to enhance the colors or change the areas in focus in an image. You

can draw attention to one part of the image using a vignette or give an ordinary photo a painterly glow. Using the Merge to HDR feature, you can combine multiple exposures to realize a photo with a wider range of tones than the camera can capture in one shot. You can also use the flexibility of smart objects and Camera Raw 4 to vary the luminosity of one photo. You can even use parts of a photo and multiple layers to create an original design. The new Vanishing Point filter enables you to remove unwanted items from a photograph or place different elements into an image while maintaining the basic perspective.

Photoshop CS3 offers more methods for altering images and more ways to be creative.

Top 100

Apply a SMART DIGITAL PHOTO FILTER for dynamic adjustments

Different lighting conditions produce different color temperatures, creating colorcasts, especially on film that is not prebalanced for the specific type of light source. Photographers often use colored lens filters to correct for the lighting differences, change the color balance in their photos, or even to create a more dramatic image. Digital images also display different color temperatures depending on the white balance settings used. You can use the Photo Filter adjustment in Photoshop to apply a traditional lens filter effect to an image whether it is digital or

scanned from film. Because Photoshop considers Photo Filter an adjustment rather than a filter, you find the Photo Filter adjustment under both the Adjustments and Adjustments Layer menus.

Using a Photo Filter adjustment can visually change the time of day in the photo, turning midday into sunset. You can also revive an image, turning a bland photo into a dramatic one, by applying a blue or violet filter across the entire image or warming a cool photo by applying a warming filter.

① Click the New Adjustment Layer button.

Note: Using the Photo Filter adjustment layer does not alter the original image until you flatten the layers.

② Click Photo Filter.

The Photo Filter dialog box appears.

③ Move the dialog box so that you can see the image.

● Make sure that Preview and Preserve Luminosity are selected.

④ Click here and select a colored filter.

⑤ Click and drag the Density slider to increase the effect if necessary.

⑥ Click OK.

The Photo Filter adjustment is applied to the entire image.

Note: You can duplicate the layer to increase the effect or change the Layer Blend mode to Hue to soften the effect.

Add a QUICK DARK VIGNETTE EFFECT
to direct the focus on the subject

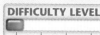
A dark vignette around the edges of a photograph is often due to the light falloff in the camera lens. However, darkening the edges of an image can also help focus the viewer's eye on the subject in the center of an image. For other images, a darkened edge can simulate the look of an old photograph. Used on a portrait, it can create a dramatic look by appearing to focus a soft light on the subject. With a landscape, you can simulate a burned-in edge, essentially enhancing the center of the image.

You can create a vignette effect in many ways with Photoshop. Most methods involve separate layers and multiple steps. This quick vignette technique uses the Lens Correction filter, almost opposite from the way it was intended, and makes adding a darkened- or lightened-edge vignette very fast. When you apply the filter as a smart filter, the effect is also completely editable even after it has been applied.

1. Open an image as a smart object or convert it using one of the methods described in Task #19.

2. Click Filter.

3. Click Distort.

4. Click Lens Correction.

The Lens Correction dialog box appears.

5. Click here to remove the grid lines.

6. Click and drag the Amount slider to the left for a dark-edge vignette effect.

   Note: You can move the Amount slider to the right to create a light-edge vignette.

7. Click and drag this slider to control how far the darkened areas extend into the photograph.

8. Click OK.

   The smart filter is applied to the image.

Add action with a simulated
MOTION BLUR

You can add a greater sense of movement to action shots by using a filter to simulate the motion of the subjects. Photoshop includes a number of blur filters, including one for motion blur. Unlike the Gaussian Blur filter, which blurs pixels in clusters, the Motion Blur filter blurs pixels in both directions along straight lines. You can choose the angle of movement and the distance in pixels that are affected by the blur in the filter dialog box to simulate both the direction and speed of motion of the subject of the photo.

The Motion Blur filter blurs the entire image, removing all details. The subject matter as well as

the background is blurred, making the photo look as though the camera and not the subject was moving when the shot was taken. By adding a layer mask filled with black to hide the motion blur, you can then selectively paint in white over certain areas to create the illusion of movement while keeping the main subject and the background in focus. Apply the filter as a smart filter on a previously converted smart object layer, and you can edit the amount of blur after applying it.

Photo © 2007 www.photospin.com

① With the image as a smart object layer (see Task #19), click Filter.

② Click Blur.

③ Click Motion Blur.

The Motion Blur dialog box appears.

④ Click and drag the straight line in the circle to rotate the angle of the motion.

⑤ Click and drag the distance slider to adjust the amount of blur.

⑥ Click OK.

The filter is applied to the smart object layer.

⑦ Press D to reset the foreground and background colors.

⑧ Click the Layer Mask icon for the smart filter.

The mask appears with a line around it, and the foreground color changes to white.

⑨ Press ⌘+Delete (Ctrl+Backspace) to fill the smart filter layer mask with black.

The motion blur effect is hidden, and the mask is filled with black.

⑩ Click the Brush tool.

⑪ Click here and click a soft-edge brush from the Brush Picker.

⑫ Paint in the image over the areas where you want the motion blur to appear.

The motion blur is applied to specific areas, and the subject appears to be moving through the background.

Did You Know?

You can also use the Wind filter for a linear motion effect. Instead of selecting the Motion Blur filter, click Filter ➔ Stylize ➔ Wind. Click From the Right or From the Left to select the direction of the movement. Click OK to close the dialog box. Then follow steps **7** to **12** in this task to selectively paint in the appropriate motion.

More Options!

After applying the Motion Blur smart filter, you can instead leave the blur over the entire image and paint back the subject and foreground to bring them back into focus. Click the mask to select it as in step **8** and press X to reverse the foreground and background colors. Paint with black over the areas that you want in focus.

Using the
NEW BLEND MODE
to stylize an image

The two new blend modes included in Photoshop CS3 called *Darker Color* and *Lighter Color* add more options for stylizing photos or designs. The new Darker Color mode displays only the one lowest value color from both the blend and base layer colors in the blended image, and, conversely, Lighter Color displays only the one highest value color. With a color layer in Darker Color blend mode, for example, only the darkest color values in the image layer below show through. In contrast, the Lighten and Darken blend modes compare all the color information in each channel of the image and thus display more gradations in the final blend for a different effect.

Applying the Darker Color or Lighter Color blend modes to a layer of color with a high contrast image layer below is particularly effective.

Start with either a color or grayscale image and add a Threshold adjustment layer to convert it to an absolute-contrast black and white. Apply the Darker or Lighter Color blend mode to a Solid Color or Gradient Fill adjustment layer to create an effect that remains editable.

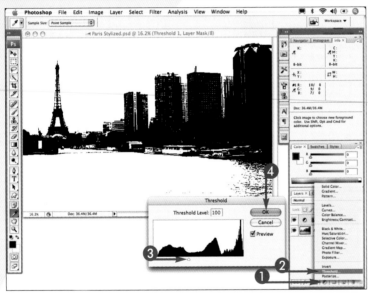

① With an image open, click the New Adjustment Layer button.

② Click Threshold.

The Threshold dialog box appears.

③ Click and drag the slider to adjust the amount for your image.

Note: The Threshold adjustment changes all color information to either black or white. Moving the slider to the right of the midpoint, 128, makes more tonal values shift to black. Moving to the left makes more tonal values turn white.

④ Click OK.

⑤ Click the New Adjustment Layer button.

⑥ Click Gradient.

Note: Clicking Solid Color instead produces a two-tone stylized effect with only one color and either white or black.

The Gradient dialog box appears.

⑦ Click here.

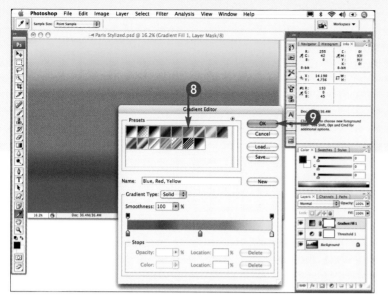

The Gradient Editor appears.

8 Click a different preset.

9 Click OK.

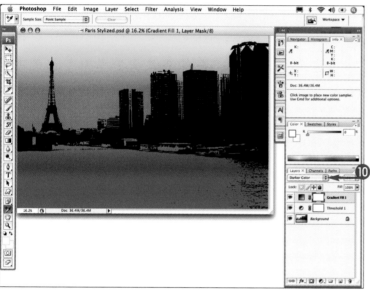

The gradient is applied as a separate adjustment layer covering the image.

10 Click here and select Darker Color to make the black areas in the image below show as black in the resulting blended image.

The gradient layer blends with the high contrast of the image.

TIPS

More Options!
You can double-click the Threshold adjustment layer or the Gradient Fill adjustment layer anytime and adjust the amount of black or the color variations to change the stylized effect.

Did You Know?
You can create your own custom gradient in the Gradient Editor. Double-click in each of the lower color stops under the gradient to open the Color Picker and select a new color.

Try It!
Instead of Darker Color, click the Blend mode arrow in the Layers palette and select Lighter Color. The image changes, applying the gradient blend to the previously black or darkest areas of the image, leaving the other areas white.

Chapter 6: Making Magic with Digital Special Effects

ALIGN AND BLEND SEPARATE PHOTOS
for the best group shot

Photoshop CS3 introduces a new Auto-Align Layers command to help you combine separate photos for panoramas or for composites. Auto-Align Layers analyzes edges and common elements in each image and brings them into alignment with each other. Not only can this tool help with registering misaligned photos when using the Merge to HDR command with exposure-bracketed photographs or for panorama stitching, but it is also perfect for combining multiple photos in group shots and getting everyone to look their best in the final photo.

You can drag all the separate images onto one of the images, making multiple layers. When you run the Auto-Align Layers command, Photoshop matches each layer with the others so that the similar shapes and forms match as much as possible. You can then add a layer mask to the layers to merge the images, erasing away the unwanted parts of each layer. For group shots, you erase the closed eyes or grimaces to combine the best of the group.

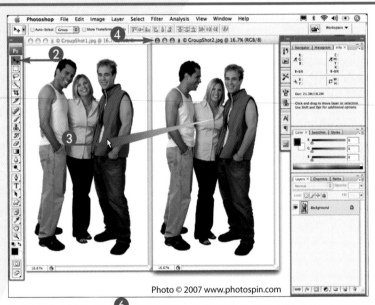

Photo © 2007 www.photospin.com

1 Open the photos to combine.

2 Click the Move tool.

3 Click and drag one photo on top of the other.

4 Click here to close the photo that you just dragged.

5 Press Shift and click each layer to select them.

6 Click Edit.

7 Click Auto-Align Layers.

The Auto-Align Layers dialog box appears.

8 Click Auto for the type of projection, depending on the elements in the photos.

9 Click OK.

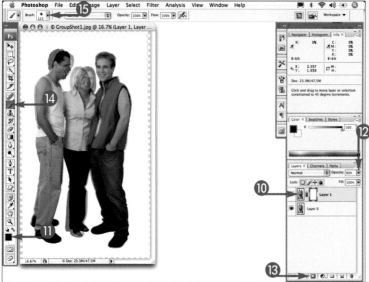

A progress bar appears, and Photoshop aligns the photos by the content.

⑩ Click the top layer to select it.

⑪ Press D to set the foreground color to black.

⑫ Click here and drag the top layer's opacity to 60% to see the shapes below.

⑬ Click here to add a layer mask to the top layer.

⑭ Click the Brush tool.

⑮ Click here and select a soft-edge brush.

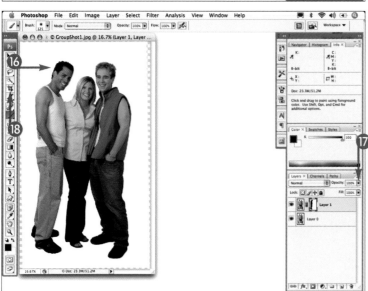

⑯ Paint with black on the top layer to show the best group shots.

Note: The top layer's mask should still be selected.

⑰ Click here and drag the top layer's opacity back to 100%.

⑱ Click the Crop tool and crop the image to final size.

The final image blends the preferred subjects from both images.

TIPS

Caution!

Make sure that the top layer's mask is still selected and that the foreground color is set to black when you paint on the photo to reveal the parts of the image on the layer below.

Did You Know?

Photoshop automatically selects one alignment projection option based on the contents of the images you are combining. You can try it and then press ⌘+Z (Ctrl+Z) to undo the auto-alignment and try a different option.

More Options!

The new Auto-Blend Layers command blends separate layers and tries to reduce or eliminate the perspective differences as well as the differences in colors or luminance without leaving a seam.

MERGE MULTIPLE RAW PHOTOS
to 32-bit HDR

Dynamic range in a photo refers to the ratio between the dark and bright areas. The human eye can adapt to different brightness levels, but the camera cannot. Using Photoshop CS3, you can merge multiple photos of the same scene but with different exposures into a High Dynamic Range (HDR) image, with luminosity levels even beyond what the human eye can see. Using Merge to HDR, the blended image can represent more shades of the colors in the visible world. Although HDR images today are used mostly

for motion pictures and special lighting effects in some high-end photography, Photoshop CS3's Merge to HDR command also opens the possibilities for photographs with more dynamic range.

Photoshop CS3 adds more support for 32-bit files than the previous version. You can now add layers and layer masks and use some of the adjustment layer types, blend modes, filters, and various tools on 32-bit images. Photoshop Extended includes a new HDR Color Picker.

OPEN MERGE TO HDR FROM THE BRIDGE

① In the Bridge, press Shift and click to select the images to merge.

② Click Tools.

③ Click Photoshop.

④ Click Merge to HDR.

*Note: Continue the steps starting with step **8** below.*

OPEN MERGE TO HDR FROM PHOTOSHOP

① In Photoshop, click File.

② Click Automate.

③ Click Merge to HDR.

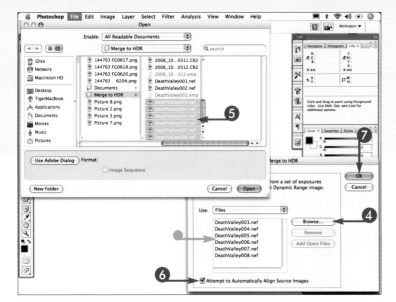

The Merge to HDR dialog box appears.

④ Click Browse.

The Open dialog box appears.

⑤ Navigate to and press Shift+click to select the images to use.

● The files appear in the list box.

⑥ Click here.

⑦ Click OK.

Photoshop opens, analyzes, and combines the images into one multilayered file.

Photoshop automatically applies the Auto-Align Layers command and crops the image.

The larger Merge to HDR dialog box appears.

⑧ Click here to deselect some of the source images if necessary.

⑨ Click and drag the slider to fit your image.

⑩ Click OK.

Photoshop merges the files into a document named Untitled_HDR.

TIPS

Did You Know?

As of today, only some monitors — such as the Eizo CG221 — and some printers — such as Canon's iPF5000, 8000, and 9000 — are capable of displaying or printing greater than 8-bit images.

Attention!

The Merge to HDR command works best on photos taken with a tripod in which nothing is moving. The aperture and ISO of the images should be the same in each photo. The shutter speed for the different exposures should vary by at least one f-stop.

Did You Know?

The *bit depth* describes how much color information exists per pixel in an image. A greater number of bits per pixel translates into greater color accuracy, with more shades of color or grays in the image.

APPLY A SPLIT-NEUTRAL DENSITY FILTER using smart objects

You may have photographed a scene with a dynamic sky, but the resulting photo did not reflect the drama that you saw. The light in the sky or a reflection of water may have created a dynamic range larger than what the camera can capture. Photographers sometimes use a split-neutral density filter on the lens to capture such a large dynamic range. Using a tripod, you can also take multiple exposures of the same scene and combine the images using Photoshop's Merge to HDR command. However, you can effectively simulate a neutral density filter or a

multiexposure photograph using a combination of Camera Raw and smart object layers.

Using two copies of a smart object layer, you can use Camera Raw 4 to edit a photograph — first to emphasize the foreground and then edit a copy to emphasize the background or sky. Then use a layer mask to combine the best exposures of both images. You can also edit each layer again before flattening and saving the final image file with a new name.

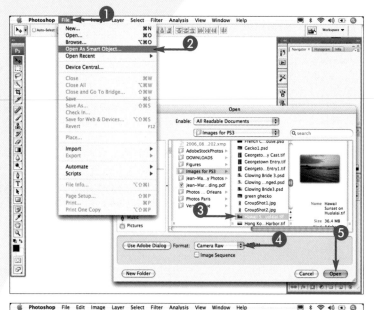

① Click File.

② Click Open As Smart Object.

The Open dialog box appears.

③ Click a file to select it.

④ Click here and select Camera Raw.

⑤ Click Open.

The Camera Raw dialog box appears.

⑥ Move the slider to simulate the best exposure for the foreground.

⑦ Click OK.

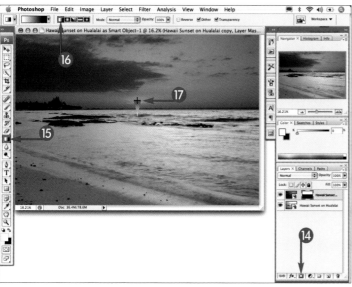

- The file is opened in Photoshop as a smart object.

⑧ Click Layer.

⑨ Click Smart Objects.

⑩ Click New Smart Object via Copy.

- The smart object layer is duplicated but not linked to the original.

⑪ Double-click the Smart Object icon on the new smart object layer.

The image opens in Camera Raw again.

⑫ Repeat steps **6** and **7**, but this time select the best exposure for the sky.

The top layer reappears.

⑬ Press D.

⑭ Click here to add a layer mask to the top layer.

⑮ Click the Gradient tool.

⑯ Click here.

⑰ Press Shift and click and drag from just above the horizon to just below the horizon.

The gradient on the mask allows the properly exposed sky from the top smart object layer to be seen on the smart object photo layer with the well-exposed foreground.

TIPS

Caution!

You must duplicate the smart object layer using the menu path Layer → Smart Objects → New Smart Object via Copy to edit each one independently. If you duplicate the smart object by dragging it over the New Layer button in the Layers palette, the smart object layers are linked to each other, and editing one edits the other at the same time.

More Options!

If the file is in the Raw format, you can start from the Bridge. Double-click the Raw file to open the Camera Raw 4 dialog box. Make your adjustments for the foreground. Press Shift and click Open Object. The file then opens as a smart object, and you can continue with the rest of the steps in the task starting at step **8**.

ADJUST DEPTH OF FIELD
with a Lens Blur filter

You can draw the attention of the viewer into the main subject of an image by controlling the depth of field, or defining the part of the image that is in focus and blurring other areas. Photographers control the depth of field by changing the aperture setting on the camera. A small opening results in a greater depth of field with more of the image in focus. A larger aperture creates an image with less depth of field and only the center of the image in focus. You can use Photoshop's blur filters to

selectively adjust the depth of field in your digital images. Use the Lens Blur filter and a white-to-black gradient on an Alpha channel to create a smooth transition from the focused areas to the out-of-focus areas in the photo. Click one area in the image to set the main focal point. Areas with the same level of gray in the Alpha channel as the selected area are now in focus. All other areas are blurred depending on the level of gray in the Alpha channel.

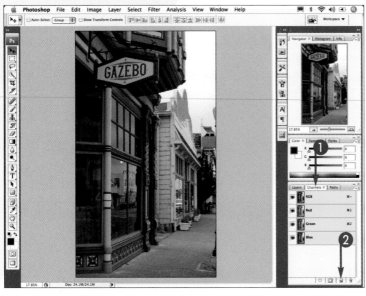

① Click the Channels tab in the Layers palette.

② Click the New Channel button to add a new black Alpha channel.

Optionally, you can press the F key once to view the photo against a gray background.

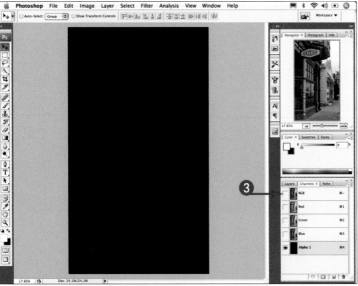

The image is covered with black, and the channel is named Alpha 1.

③ Click the Visibility box for the RGB channel to see the image.

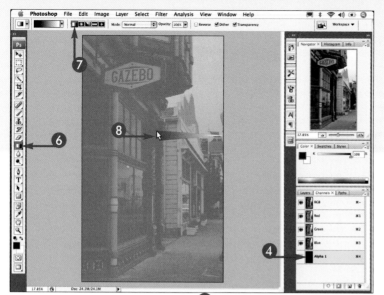

All the channels are visible, and a red mask covers the image.

④ Click the Alpha 1 channel to highlight it.

⑤ Press D to select the default foreground and background colors.

⑥ Click the Gradient tool.

⑦ Click the Linear gradient.

⑧ Press and hold the Shift key as you click and drag in the image from the background toward the foreground.

The red mask area appears as a red gradient.

⑨ Click the RGB channel to highlight it.

⑩ Click Filter.

⑪ Click Blur.

⑫ Click Lens Blur.

TIPS

More Options!

You can create a selection in the image and click Select → Save Selection. Type a name in the data field in the Save Selection dialog box. Click OK. Hide the visibility of the new channel, click the RGB channel in the Layers palette, and then click the Layers tab. Apply the Lens Blur filter, and everything in the selection remains in focus.

Try This!

You can also create a channel with two selections, one for the main subject and the second for an area slightly farther in the background. Fill the first selection with white and the second with a light gray. Apply the Lens Blur filter with this channel as the source. Your image now has areas with three distinct levels of focus.

Chapter 6: Making Magic with Digital Special Effects

ADJUST DEPTH OF FIELD
with a Lens Blur filter

Photoshop includes other blur filters. All the blur filters can soften or blur either a selected area or the entire image. These filters smooth the transitions between areas of contrast from hard edges or shaded areas by averaging the pixels that are juxtaposed to any lines or edges in an image. The Lens Blur filter works best for creating or simulating depth of field in a photo because it uses a depth map to determine the position of the pixels to blur. You can set the specific area to start blurring the focus in the image

by specifying the source for the depth map. Using the Lens Blur filter with a separate Alpha channel or a layer mask as the source enables you to specify exactly what is in sharp focus and how much depth of field to apply. The Lens Blur filter also enables you to determine the shape of the iris to control how the blur appears. By changing the shape, curvature, or rotation of the iris in the Lens Blur dialog box, you control the look of the Lens Blur filter.

The Lens Blur dialog box appears.

⑬ Click and drag all the sliders to the left to remove any blur effect.

⑭ Click here and select Alpha 1.

⑮ Click the main subject in the image to assign the point of focus.

⑯ Click and drag the Radius slider to the right to blur the background.

⑰ Click and drag the Blur Focal Distance slider to adjust the point of focus if necessary.

Note: *The Blur Focal Distance number corresponds to the level of gray at the targeted point in the Alpha channel.*

⑱ Click OK.

The Lens Blur filter is applied to the image.

⑲ Click the Visibility icon on the Alpha 1 channel to deselect it and hide the red mask.

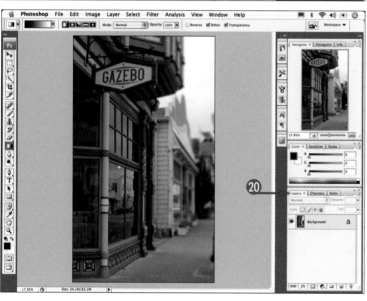

⑳ Click the Layers tab.

The main subject in the image is sharp while the rest of the image gradually blurs out of focus as it gets farther away from the focal point.

TIPS

Attention!

Film grain and noise are removed when the Lens Blur filter is applied. You can replace some of the noise and make the image look more realistic. First, zoom in to see the image at 100 percent. Click and drag the Amount slider in the Noise section of the Lens Blur dialog box until the image appears less changed and click OK.

Did You Know?

Applying a Lens Blur filter rather than a Gaussian Blur filter preserves more of the geometric shapes in the original image. Highlights in the image also reflect the Shape setting that is chosen in the Iris section of the Lens Blur dialog box. You can smooth the edges of the iris and rotate it by changing the Blade Curvature and Rotation settings.

CREATE A SILHOUETTE
for a custom design

Many advertising layouts are designed with a silhouetted person or object against a plain, colored background. You can easily create a similar design by making a selection in a photograph and using that selection in a background document. The silhouette design can be very effective, not only as an advertising piece but also as a business card, a greeting card, a postcard, or an original logo.

Not all objects in a photograph can be used as a silhouette. The subject needs to have a detailed

enough shape when contrasted against a background to not only stand out but also be recognizable. People or objects that are angled or positioned parallel to the plane of the photograph often work best. The size of the object is not important because you can transform and resize the silhouetted item to fit your design. You can use just one silhouette or combine any number of objects from various photos and place these on any colored background. Just add some text to complete the design.

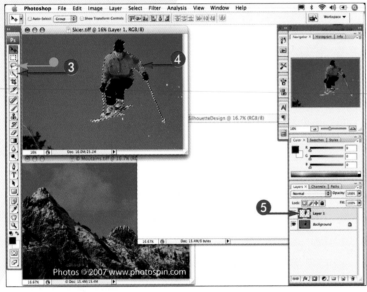

① Open the photos with the objects for the silhouettes and a new blank document with the width, height, and resolution set for the custom layout.

② Press D to set the foreground color to black.

③ Click the Quick Select tool.

● Optionally, you can click the Lasso tool to select the subject.

④ Click and drag a detailed selection around the subject as in Task #16.

⑤ Press ⌘+J (Ctrl+J) to put the selected area on its own layer.

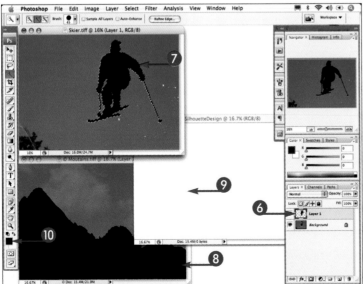

⑥ Press ⌘ (Ctrl) and click the Layer 1 thumbnail to target the selection.

⑦ Press Option+Delete (Alt+Backspace) to fill the selection with black.

⑧ Repeat steps **3** to **7** for any additional photos.

⑨ Click the blank document to select it.

⑩ Click the foreground color in the toolbox.

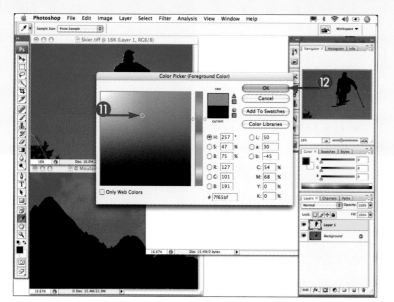

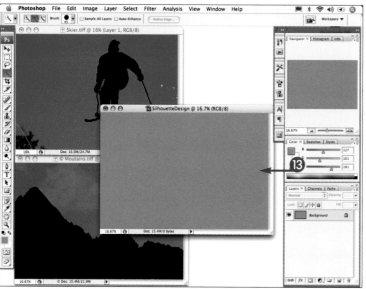

The Color Picker appears.

⑪ Click to select a color for the new document.

⑫ Click OK.

Note: *The Warning triangle next to the selected color is an Out-of-Gamut alert indicating that a color will not print exactly as seen on the screen.*

59

DIFFICULTY LEVEL

⑬ With the blank document selected, press Option+Delete (Alt+Backspace) to fill the layer with the new foreground color.

The new document fills with the foreground color.

More Options!

Pressing ⌘+Tab (Ctrl+Tab) enables you to cycle through all open documents. You can select the one that you need to work on without clicking and dragging the others out of the way in the document window.

Did You Know?

You can view all the open documents at once by clicking Window → Arrange and selecting Tile Horizontally or Tile Vertically. Clicking Window → Arrange → Cascade makes the documents align to occupy the least amount of space.

More Options!

Press ⌘++ (Ctrl++) to enlarge the preview. Press ⌘+- (Ctrl+-) to reduce the preview. Press ⌘+spacebar (Ctrl+spacebar) and click to zoom in even with another tool selected. Press Option+spacebar (Alt+spacebar) and click to zoom out.

CREATE A SILHOUETTE
for a custom design

The silhouette technique can be used in a variety of ways. It can be the main part of the design or a secondary element in the overall piece. A wedding thank-you note, for example, may have a small silhouette of the couple kissing on the inside or back of the card.

You can make variations to the silhouette and the background depending on the purpose of the piece. Highlighting specific areas such as a bracelet or a belt adds dimension and focus to the silhouette. Select these areas as the first step. Jump the

selections to a separate layer and fill them with white. Then continue creating the silhouetted form. Place the highlights layer above the silhouette layer and merge these two layers. For a more subtle overall effect, you can apply a gradient to the background layer instead of using a solid color. Place the most important part of the silhouette over the lightest part of the gradient. As the gradient gets lighter, the silhouette stands out more due to the increased contrast.

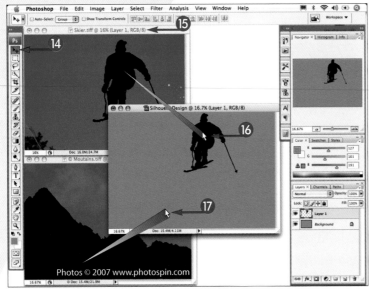

⑭ Click the Move tool.

⑮ Click one of the photos to activate it.

⑯ Click the black silhouette and drag it onto the new document.

⑰ Repeat steps **14** to **16** for any additional silhouettes.

● The silhouettes appear on separate layers in the new document.

⑱ Click Auto-Select.

⑲ Click Show Transform Controls.

⑳ Click the Close button to close each photo.

Note: Do not save the changes to the images when the dialog box appears.

㉑ Press ⌘++ (Ctrl++) to enlarge the design document.

22 Press Shift and click and drag the corner of the transformation anchors to resize this silhouette.

23 Click the silhouette and drag it into position.

24 Press Return (Enter) to apply the transformation.

25 Repeat steps **22** to **24** for any additional silhouettes.

ADD TEXT TO YOUR DESIGN

26 Click the Type tool.

27 Select a color, font, and size in the Type tool's Options bar.

28 Click in the image and type some text.

29 Press Return (Enter) to apply the text.

APPLY A GRADIENT

30 Click the Background layer.

31 Click the Gradient tool.

32 Click here.

33 Click with the Color Picker eyedropper in the main color of the design to select that color and click OK.

34 Press Shift+click and drag in the image to create a gradient background.

TIPS

More Options!

Pressing ⌘+T (Ctrl+T) brings up the Transformation controls. You can press Return (Enter) instead of clicking the Commit button on the Options bar to apply the transformation. You can press Esc to cancel the transformation.

Did You Know?

Selecting the Auto-Select Layer and the Auto-Select Groups check boxes on the Options bar enables you to click an item in a multilayered document and automatically select the layer that contains the item.

Try This!

Selecting the Show Transform Controls check box on the Options bar makes the transformation anchors appear. You can then click and drag the corner anchors to resize without clicking the Edit menu and selecting Free Transform.

BECOME A DIGITAL ARCHITECT
with the Vanishing Point filter

The Vanishing Point filter helps Photoshop recognize the third dimension of objects so that you can manipulate items in perspective. Using the Grid tool, you create a grid over a rectangular area and then extend the grid by pulling on the anchor points. You can then pull a secondary plane around 90 degree corners. With Photoshop CS3, you can now drag out a secondary plane and rotate it by any amount. After the grids or perspective planes are defined, you can change the look of the image by erasing items, copying objects from one area of the image to

another, or adding items from other images, all while keeping the perspective in the original photo. You can expand a building to make it look taller than it is, erase or add windows to a structure, add a cover design to the photo of an open book, or even add signs on any building.

The first grid must be accurate. A blue grid shows a correct perspective plane. A red or yellow grid must be must adjusted using the anchor points until the grid turns blue.

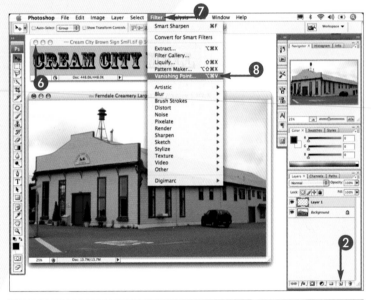

1. Open a main image.
2. Click here to add a new layer.
3. Open a second image to be used on the main image.
4. Press ⌘+A (Ctrl+A) to select the entire second image.

   Note: You can select just an area.
5. Press ⌘+C (Ctrl+C).
6. Click here to close the second image.
7. Click Filter.
8. Click Vanishing Point.

The Vanishing Point dialog box appears.

- The Create Plane tool is automatically selected.

9. Click four corners of an area that shows the perspective of the photo to create a blue grid.
10. Click the Edit Plane tool.
11. Click and drag the center points of the grid to extend the plane.
12. Press ⌘ (Ctrl) and click and drag a center point to create a perpendicular plane.

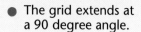

- The grid extends at a 90 degree angle.

⑬ Press Option+click (Alt+click) and drag a center point to swing the plane into position.

The perspective plane swings around and aligns at a different angle.

⑭ Press ⌘+V (Ctrl+V).

- The pasted image appears in a corner of the Vanishing Point dialog box.

⑮ Click and drag the second image over the perspective plane.

The second image snaps into perspective on the plane.

⑯ Click the Transform tool.

⑰ Press Shift+click and drag the corners of the second image to adjust it into position.

⑱ Click OK.

The additions in perspective are applied.

TIPS

Did You Know?

When you are in the Vanishing Point dialog box, you can use the Zoom tool to enlarge the area that you want to select. To zoom in as you are placing or adjusting the anchor points, press and hold X.

Important!

You can increase the size of the building beyond the boundaries of the existing photo. First, increase the canvas size by clicking Image → Canvas Size and adding width or height to one side of the existing image.

Caution!

When you plan to copy an item or a layer from one photo to paste into another in perspective, be sure to copy the item first to save it to the Clipboard *before* you choose the Vanishing Point filter.

Chapter 7

Designing with Text Effects

If a picture is worth a thousand words, then a picture with words has even more persuasive powers. Although Photoshop CS3 is not a page-layout application, you can add text to photographs for added impact or to create an original design. You can also add special text effects to give personality to the words or even use the words alone to create the design.

With Photoshop, you can apply effects to text in more creative ways and more quickly than is possible using traditional tools. Not only can you see the end result instantly, but you also have complete creative freedom to make changes without wasting any paper or ink. By combining layer styles, patterns, colors, and fonts, you can create type with just the right look for your project. You can use text on

images and make the words appear as part of the photograph and, conversely, make the photo appear as part of the text.

When you type in Photoshop, the text is placed on a type layer as *vectors,* or mathematically defined shapes that describe the letters, numbers, and symbols of a typeface. You can scale or resize the words, edit the text, and apply many layer effects to the text while preserving the crisp edges. Some commands and tools, however, require the type to be *rasterized,* or converted to a normal layer filled with pixels. The filter effects and painting tools and the perspective and distort commands can only work after the type has been rasterized. After the type layer has been converted, the text is no longer editable.

Top 100

Add a
DOUBLE-NEON GLOW
to text for a unique design

You can easily give any text a double-neon glow effect using a variation of a technique taught by Colin Smith of PhotoshopCAFÉ. Colin is an award-winning Photoshop and Flash designer and teaches the new media through his instructional videos called the *Photoshop Secrets* video training series. He also writes the CAFÉ cup, a free subscription newsletter, and runs the PhotoshopCAFE.com Web site, a powerful resource for Photoshop-related news.

The double-neon glow can be very effective for creating album or Web page titles. Set against a dark background, the glowing letters quickly capture your viewer's attention. You can easily change the way the letters glow on the screen by changing the background layer color or adding a gradient background. The double-glow effect surrounding the letters can be varied anytime and changed by simply double-clicking the effect icon in the Layers palette to reopen the Layer Style dialog box. By keeping the text as a type layer, you can edit the text and maintain the glow, so you can use the double-glow technique for multiple applications.

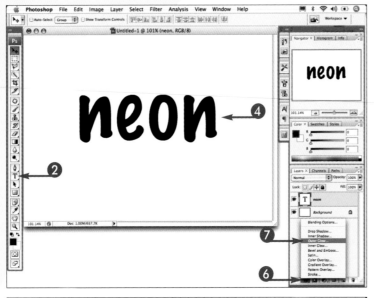

① Open a new blank document.

② Click the Type tool.

③ Select the font family, style, and size in the Options bar.

④ Click in the image and type your text.

⑤ Press Return (Enter) to commit the type.

⑥ Click the Layer Style button.

⑦ Click Outer Glow.

The Layer Style dialog box appears.

● Move the dialog box so that you can see the text.

⑧ Click and drag to increase the spread to about 13%.

⑨ Click and drag to increase the size to about 16 pixels.

⑩ Click Drop Shadow.

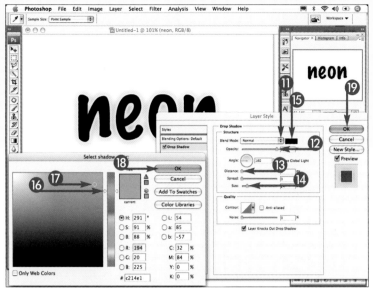

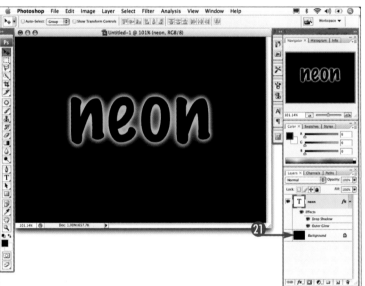

The dialog box changes.

⓫ Click here and select Normal.

⓬ Click and drag the Opacity slider to 100%.

⓭ Click and drag the distance to 0 pixels.

⓮ Increase the size of the glow to about 24.

⓯ Click here.

The Select Shadow Color dialog box appears.

⓰ Click and drag the color slider.

⓱ Click in the color box to select a glow color.

⓲ Click OK.

⓳ Click OK.

⓴ Press D to reset the default foreground color to black.

㉑ Click the Background layer to select it.

㉒ Press Option+Delete (Alt+Backspace) to fill the background with black.

㉓ Repeat steps **6** to **19** to change the color or size of the double glow.

The text appears with a neon glow against a dark background.

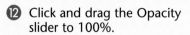

61

DIFFICULTY LEVEL

TIPS

Attention!

The double-neon glow technique works best on a dark background; however, it does not need to be black. You can also select the Gradient tool and click and drag across the Background layer to create a gradient color fill.

Keyboard Shortcuts!

With the Type tool selected, pressing Return (Enter) moves the cursor to the next line and pressing Enter or ⌘+Return (Ctrl+Enter) applies the type or any transformations. Pressing Esc cancels the Type layer.

Try This!

Type some text with the Type tool. Before clicking the Commit button, press and hold ⌘ (Ctrl) to bring up the transformation anchor points. Click and drag the anchors while pressing ⌘ (Ctrl) to transform the type.

Create a
CUSTOM WATERMARK
to protect your images

If you upload your proofs to a Web site for client approval or if you sell your digital artwork online, you want people to see the images but not to use the files without your permission. You can add a custom watermark with a transparent look to any image to protect it and still keep the image visible.

A custom watermark can be as simple as your name and the copyright symbol. After typing your name on a type layer and adding a large copyright symbol as

a shape layer, you can add any kind of bevel or embossed style to your personalized watermark. You can even copy the two layers to another photo to apply the same custom watermark. To give a transparent look to each layer, you lower the Fill opacity, which only affects the fill pixels, leaving the beveled areas appearing like a glass overlay. You can also use the same technique to give a transparent look to any text, shape, or other layer on any image.

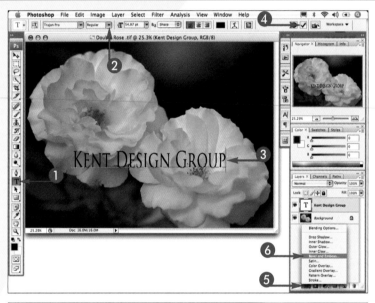

① With the image open, click the Type tool.

② Select the font family, style, and size in the Options bar.

③ Click in the image and type the text for your watermark, such as your name or company name.

④ Click the Commit button.

⑤ Click the Layer Style button.

⑥ Click Bevel and Emboss.

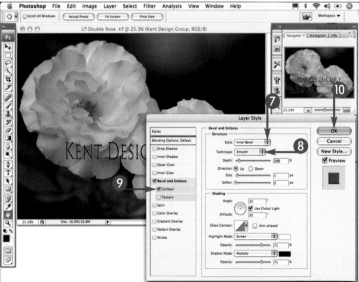

The Layer Style dialog box appears.

⑦ Click here and select Inner Bevel.

⑧ Click here and select Smooth.

⑨ Click Contour.

⑩ Click OK.

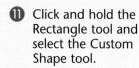

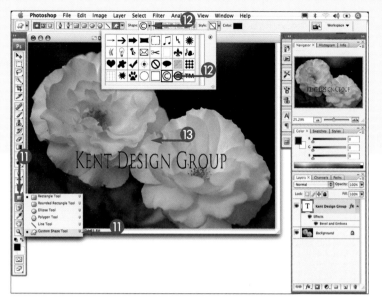

11 Click and hold the Rectangle tool and select the Custom Shape tool.

12 Click here and select the copyright symbol.

13 Press Shift and click and drag in the photo to create a copyright symbol.

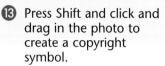

The copyright symbol appears on the image and as a shape layer in the Layers palette.

14 Press Option (Alt) and click and drag the Layer Style icon to the shape layer to copy the effect.

The same emboss style is applied to the copyright symbol.

15 Double-click in the Fill data field and type **0**.

16 Click the type layer to select it and repeat step **15**.

The name and copyright symbol appear embossed on the image.

TIPS

Caution!

There are three options on the Options bar for the Custom Shape tool. When you select the Shape tool for the copyright symbol, make sure that the Shape Layer button is highlighted on the Options bar rather than the Paths or Fill Pixels button.

Did You Know?

The Layers palette includes two types of sliders. The Opacity slider affects the visibility of both the filled pixels and the layer style. The Fill slider affects only the transparency of the filled pixels without changing any style that is applied.

Try This!

Double-clicking the Type thumbnail in the Layers palette selects and highlights all the type on that layer. Double-clicking the blank space next to the name of a layer brings up the Layer Style dialog box.

FILL ANY SHAPE WITH TEXT

to create unique effects

#63

DIFFICULTY LEVEL

In Photoshop, you can type text in several ways. Any text that is typed is placed on a type layer, retaining its vector-based outlines so that you can scale, skew, or rotate it to fit your design. With the Type tool selected, place the cursor anywhere in an image and type the text or type the text so that it flows along the edge of a path.

You can also type text as a paragraph, either horizontally or vertically, and control the flow of the characters within a bounding box. For text in a

rectangular shape, you can use the Type tool to drag diagonally and define a bounding area and then click and type the text. Typing text as a paragraph is useful for creating brochures, scrapbooks, or various design projects. The bounding box, however, is not limited to the rectangular shape created by dragging the Type tool. You can also drag out any shape selected from the Custom Shape Picker using the Custom Shape tool. You can then fill the shape with paragraph text to create unique visual effects.

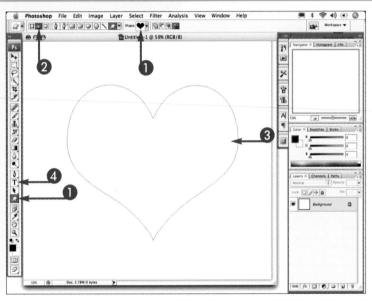

① Click the Custom Shape tool and select a custom shape as in steps **11** and **12** in Task #62.

② Click the Paths button.

③ Click and drag in the image to create the shape.

Note: Press Shift to constrain the shape and press the spacebar to reposition the shape.

④ Click the Type tool.

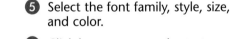

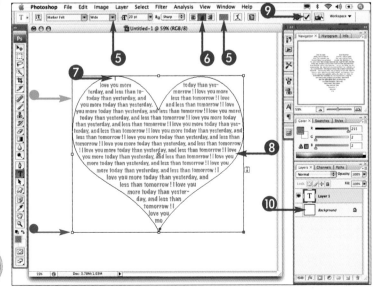

⑤ Select the font family, style, size, and color.

⑥ Click here to center the text.

⑦ Click inside the shape.

● A bounding box surrounds the shape.

⑧ Type the text until the shape is full.

● You can click and drag the anchor points around the shape to alter the form.

⑨ Click the Commit button.

⑩ Click here to view the text without the outline of the shape.

WARP TYPE
to emphasize the words

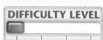

You can create many different effects with type by warping the letters into various shapes. If you warp text using the Warp command found under the Edit and Transform menu after rasterizing the type layer, or turning the layer into pixels, the letters lose their sharp edges and appear fuzzy. Using the Warp Text feature of Photoshop gives text a completely new look and helps it remain sharp-edged and editable.

After you type the text, you use the Warp Text dialog box to change it. You can select from a variety of

warp styles and use the sliders to alter the look. You can control the direction of the warp as well as size of the letters. Because the warp style is an attribute of the type layer, you can change the style at any time by reselecting the layer with the Type tool and opening the Warp Text dialog box. As long as the text is on an editable type layer, you can apply any layer styles before or after warping the text.

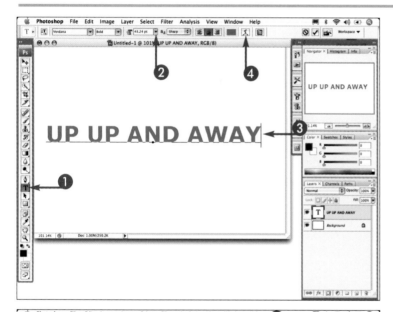

① In a new blank document, click the Type tool.

② Select the font family, style, size, justification, and color.

③ Click in the document and type the text.

④ Click the Warp Text button.

The Warp Text dialog box appears.

⑤ Move the dialog box so that you can see the type.

⑥ Click here and select a warp style.

The text matches the style selected.

⑦ Click and drag each of the sliders to vary the effect.

⑧ Click OK.

⑨ Click the Commit button.

The warp and changes to the text are committed.

ADD PERSPECTIVE TO TYPE
and keep it sharp

When you warp a type layer, the letters always bend the shape to some degree, even if you set the Bend slider to 0. Although using the Perspective function found under the Edit menu's Transform submenu more accurately gives the illusion of text disappearing into the distance, this function is unavailable for a type layer. If you rasterize the layer and turn the letters into pixels to use the Perspective transformation, the characters blur as you change the angles. You can, however, add realistic perspective to type and preserve the crisp edges by converting the type layer to a shape layer.

Converting type to shapes changes the type layer into a layer with a colored fill and a linked vector mask showing the outline of the letters. The outline is actually a temporary path and appears in the Paths palette as well. The text is no longer editable, but you can alter the vector mask, add layer styles, and use all the transformation tools to change the look.

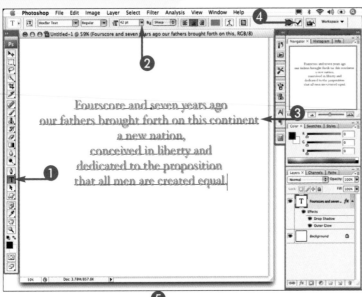

1. In a new blank document, click the Type tool.

2. Select the font family, style, size, justification, and color.

3. Click in the image and type the text.

4. Click the Commit button.

5. Click Layer.

6. Click Type.

7. Click Convert to Shape.

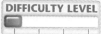

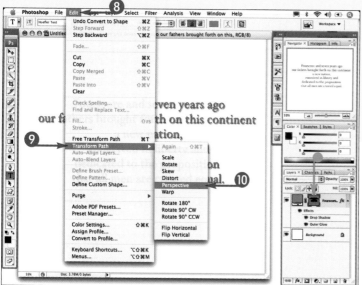

● The type layer in the Layers palette changes to a fill and vector mask.

❽ Click Edit.

❾ Click Transform Path.

❿ Click Perspective.

The text has a bounding box with anchor points.

⓫ Click one of the top corner anchors and drag toward the center top anchor.

The text appears to be lying down on a perspective plane.

⓬ Click the Commit button.

The text retains its sharp edges even as it appears in a perspective plane.

⓭ Click the Background layer to view the text without the mask outline.

TIPS

More Options!

You can also click one of the top or bottom corner anchors and drag straight up or straight down to create a vertical perspective. The letters seem to disappear into the distance in a vertical position.

Try This!

When you need to select the Type tool to edit type, double-click the *T* in the type layer thumbnail in the Layers palette. The type on the layer is highlighted, and the Type tool is automatically selected.

Try This!

You can edit type with another tool selected. Double-click the *T* in the type layer, and the Type tool and options are temporarily selected. Or click the Character palette button and make any type changes directly in that palette.

Make your
TEXT FOLLOW ANY PATH

You can make text move along an angled line or curve and swoop in any direction to create an original design. By creating an angled path with the Pen tool or a curved path with the Freeform Pen tool, you can place the Type tool cursor on the path and type the text. The text flows along the path, starting from the insertion point. Another option is to create a shape using the Shape tool and place the text around the edges of the shape. You can also use any object

in a photograph to create the path. When you add the text, it flows along the edges of the object in the photo, creating a sophisticated design.

You can use any selection tool to make a selection around the object. Convert the selection to a complex working path using the selections in the Paths palette's pop-up menu. The text remains on a type layer, so you can change or add words or style and color the letters.

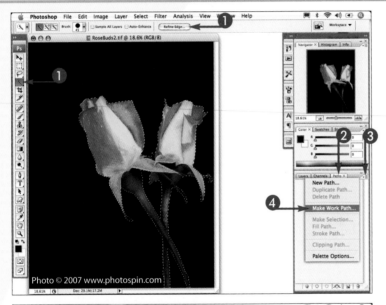

① Use the Quick Select tool and Refine Edge palette to make a selection around the image as in Task #16.

② Click the Paths tab.

③ Click here.

④ Click Make Work Path.

The Make Work Path dialog box appears.

⑤ Type **5**.

Note: For a more detailed path, type a smaller number to have more control points on the path.

⑥ Click OK.

The dotted selection lines disappear, and a new path appears in the Paths palette.

⑦ Click the Type tool.

⑧ Select the font family, style, size, and color.

⑨ Click the path and type the text.

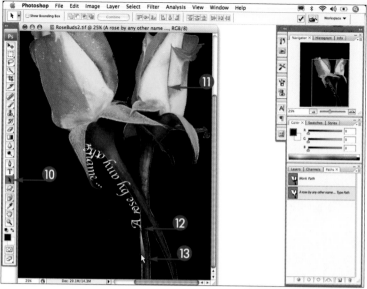

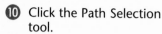

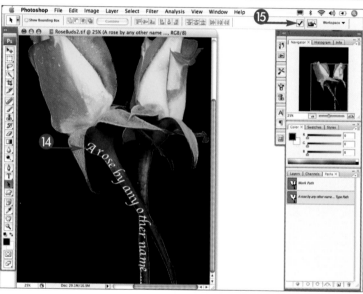

The text follows the path, and a type path appears in the Paths palette.

⑩ Click the Path Selection tool.

⑪ Press ⌘+spacebar (Ctrl+spacebar) and click the image to zoom in.

⑫ Click the small *X* at the beginning of the text.

The cursor changes to an I-beam with a small black arrow.

⑬ Drag along the path to reposition the text.

⑭ Drag the cursor across the path to put the text on the other side of the path.

⑮ Click here to dismiss the target path and commit the changes.

The type now follows the path line on the subject.

⑯ Press Option+spacebar (Alt+spacebar) to zoom out.

TIPS

Did You Know?
A small *X* indicates the beginning of the text on a path, and a small *O* indicates the end of the text. If the text is center-aligned, a small diamond shape designates the center.

Try This!
On sharp curves, letters may appear on top of each other. Click Window → Character to open the Character palette. Select the letters and adjust the tracking in the Character palette or click between the letters and adjust the kerning.

Try This!
To adjust kerning, click between two letters and press Option (Alt) and the right or left arrows. To adjust tracking, select a group of letters and press Option (Alt) and the right or left arrows.

Create eye-catching
PHOTO-FILLED TITLES

You can easily create mood-inspiring or memory-evoking titles for a photo or album page by making a photograph fill the letters. Photoshop CS3 includes two kinds of Type tools: the Horizontal and Vertical Type tools and the Horizontal and Vertical Type Mask tools. When you use the Type Mask tools, Photoshop automatically creates a selection in the shape of the letters. However, using the regular Type tools gives you more control over the design and makes it easier to see the area of the photo that will be cut out by the letters.

Filling text or any other object with a photograph or other image is one of the many collage and masking techniques in Photoshop. You type text and use a clipping mask to clip the photograph so that it only shows through the letters. Because the letters are on an editable type layer, you can change the text even after the letters are filled with the image. You can also add a drop shadow or emboss to the type layer to make the letters stand out.

① Open a photograph and rearrange the workspace as in Task #3 to increase the image space, leaving the Layers palette open.

② Click the Type tool.

③ Select the font family, style, justification, and size.

   Note: Thick sans serif fonts work best for this effect.

④ Click in the image and type the text.

⑤ Press ⌘ (Ctrl) and click and drag the transformation anchors to stretch the type.

⑥ Click the Commit button.

⑦ Click and drag the Background layer over the New Layer button to duplicate it.

⑧ Click and drag the Background copy layer above the type layer.

⑨ Click Layer.

⑩ Click Create Clipping Mask.

#67

● The Background copy layer is indented with an arrow in the Layers palette, but the image does not change.

⑪ Click here to create a new blank layer named Layer 1.

⑫ Click and drag the new blank layer below the type layer.

⑬ Press D to reset the default colors.

⑭ Press ⌘+Delete (Ctrl+Backspace) to fill the layer with white.

The photo appears to fill the letters on a white background.

⑮ Click the Move tool.

⑯ Click the Background copy layer to select it.

⑰ Click and drag in the image to move the photo into position inside the letters.

The photo is repositioned within the letters, creating an attractive photo title.

Optionally, you can click the type layer and click the Layer Styles button to add a drop shadow.

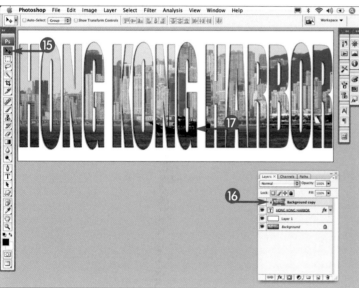

TIPS

More Options!

You can also change the type attributes using the Character palette. Click Window → Character to open the palette. Place the cursor over any of the settings to activate the scrubby sliders. Move the cursor to change the settings.

Attention!

Be sure to highlight the Background copy layer, which must be above the type layer, when you create the clipping mask. Changing the stacking order of the layers after a clipping mask has been applied can remove the clipping mask.

More Options!

You can create a clipping mask using two different keyboard shortcuts. Press Option (Alt) and click between the two layers in the Layers palette or press ⌘+Option+G (Ctrl+Alt+G).

BLEND TEXT
into a photograph creatively

When you type on a photograph, you can reduce the opacity of the type layer to make the letters fade into the image in a uniform manner. For a more interesting effect, use the Blending options in the Layer Style dialog box to give the illusion of the text disappearing behind different elements in the photograph. You can make the letters disappear behind clouds or trees, blend parts of the letters into a mountain, or create a variety of different effects using the colors from the underlying layer and the Blending options for the text layer.

The Layer Style dialog box includes Blending Options sliders for both the active layer and the underlying layer. The sliders determine which pixels appear through the active layer and which are hidden, based on the brightness of the pixels. You can make the text blend even more smoothly with the underlying photo by splitting the sliders and in effect partially blending some of the pixels in the tonal range.

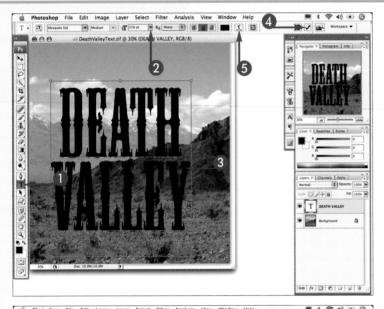

1 With the image open, click the Type tool.

2 Select the font family, style, size, and color.

3 Click in the image and type the text.

4 Click the Commit button.

5 Click the Warp Text button.

The Warp Text dialog box appears.

● Move the dialog box so that you can see the text.

6 Click here and select a warp style.

7 Click and drag the sliders to adjust the style.

8 Click OK.

9 Click here and select Blending Options.

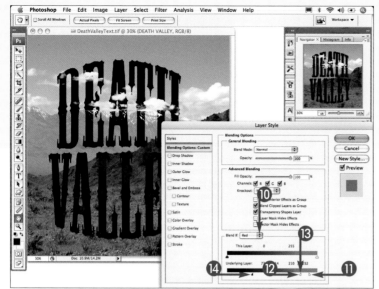

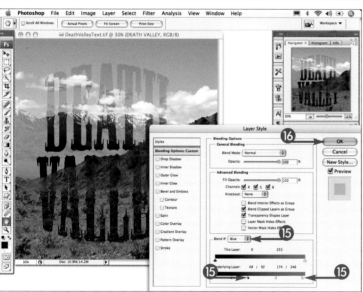

⑩ Click here and select Red.

⑪ Click and drag this white slider slightly to the left to make the lightest values in the underlying photo appear through the text.

⑫ Press Option (Alt) and click and drag the left half more to the left, separating the slider halves.

⑬ Click and drag the slider halves to vary the areas of the photo that blend with the text.

⑭ Repeat steps **11** to **13** using the black slider for the underlying layer to make the darkest values of the underlying photo appear through the text.

⑮ Repeat steps **10** to **14** for Green and Blue until the text blends with the elements in the photograph.

⑯ Click OK.

The text disappears behind some areas in the photo and shows through other parts, depending on the color values in the image.

TIPS

Did You Know?
Splitting the white highlight or the black shadow sliders for the underlying layer defines a range of partially blended or composite pixels and softens the transitions as the text is blended with the background photo.

Try This!
You can also view the Layer Style dialog box by clicking Layer → Layer Style → Blending Option or by double-clicking in the empty space next to the layer name in the Layers palette.

More Options!
You can add a bevel or emboss or any of the other layer styles to the letters at any time. Open the Layer Style dialog box and click any of the styles to see and apply the effect.

Create an amazing
COLORED SHADOW

When you apply a drop shadow to text using a Layer Style drop shadow, the shadow is gray. Actual shadows of text or other objects are not gray and do not have the same opacity on different objects. Shadows reflect the colors of the objects they cover. Selecting another color for the shadow in the Layer Style dialog box gives the shadow an unnatural and uniform color.

You can apply a drop shadow with the same colors that occur in the real world by using a selection and a Brightness/Contrast adjustment. Then by linking

the shadow layer to the text layer, you can reposition the text in the image, and the shadow follows, automatically adjusting itself for colors in the image below.

You can use the same technique to add a realistic shadow to any object in an image. Add depth to natural light shadows under a tree or increase the shadow of a person in a sunlit photo. The greater the number of colors and textures affected by the shadow, the more natural your colored shadow appears.

Photo © 2007 www.photospin.com

① Click the Type tool.

② Select the font family, style, size, and color.

③ Click in the image and type the text.

④ Click the Commit button.

⑤ Press ⌘+click (Ctrl+click) the type layer thumbnail to select the letters.

⑥ Click Select.

⑦ Click Modify.

⑧ Click Feather.

The Feather Selection dialog box appears.

⑨ Click in the data field and type **10**.

Note: The size of the feather radius depends on the size of the image.

⑩ Click OK.

⑪ Click the Type tool.

⑫ Press the right arrow key several times and the down arrow key several times.

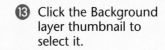

The selection marquee moves down and to the right.

⑬ Click the Background layer thumbnail to select it.

⑭ Click the New Adjustment Layer button.

⑮ Click Brightness/Contrast.

The Brightness/Contrast dialog box appears, and the selection marquee is hidden.

⑯ Move the dialog box so that you can see the image.

⑰ Click and drag the Brightness slider to the left to create the drop shadow.

⑱ Click OK.

The text can now be moved around the photo, and the shadow follows, adjusting automatically to the colors below it.

TIPS

More Options!

Press Shift and click the type layer and the adjustment layer in the Layers palette to select them both. Then click the Link Layers button in the Layers palette to link the layers for the text and the shadow together. Click the Move tool and reposition the text. The shadow follows the text around the image.

Did You Know?

You can quickly change the alignment of type using keyboard shortcuts. Click in the type and press Shift+⌘+L (Shift+Ctrl+L) to align left; press Shift+⌘+R (Shift+Ctrl+R) to align right; and press Shift+⌘+C (Shift+Ctrl+C) to align center.

WEAVE TEXT AND GRAPHICS
for intriguing designs

You can create a design using type as the central element by changing the letter styles and size, adding layer effects, warping the text, or adding perspective. You can also make the individual letters interweave and interact with each other to add more interest to any project. By converting type layers to shapes and overlapping them, you can make some of the areas transparent to the background, creating new design elements. Add a shape to the text, make the letters intertwine with the shape, and you can create eye-catching logos or page titles.

When you convert a type layer to a shape, the text is no longer editable. However, you can still move individual letters. You can transform, warp, and resize one letter at a time or a group of letters. You can also add layer styles to the grouped design elements and change the look completely. Because the letters and shapes are all on one layer, the color and any layer styles that you use are applied to all the elements on the layer. Flatten the layers as a final step in creating the design.

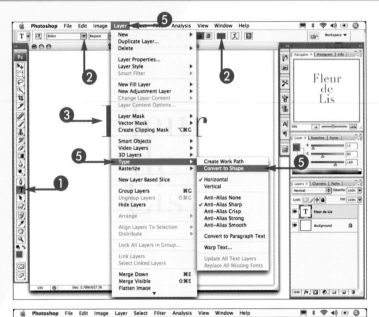

① In a new blank document, click the Type tool.

② Select the font, size, and color.

③ Click in the document and type the text.

④ Press Enter (Shift+Enter) to commit the type.

⑤ Click Layer → Type → Convert to Shape.

● The type layer changes to a fill layer and a vector mask.

⑥ Click the Path Selection tool.

⑦ Click and drag over the middle line of text to select it.

⑧ Click and drag the line up to overlap the first line of text.

⑨ Click the Exclude Overlapping Shape Areas button.

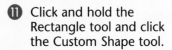

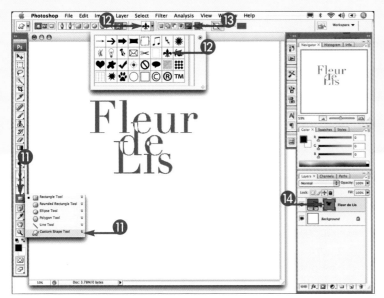

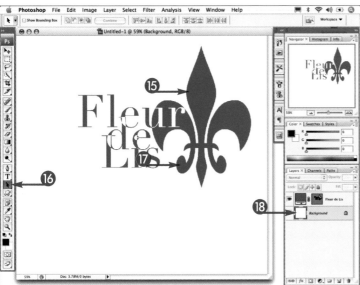

The areas of text that overlap are reversed out.

⑩ Repeat steps **7** to **9** for other lines of text.

⑪ Click and hold the Rectangle tool and click the Custom Shape tool.

⑫ Click here and click a shape to select it.

⑬ Click the Exclude Overlapping Shape Areas button.

⑭ Make sure that the vector mask thumbnail in the Layers palette is selected.

⑮ Click and drag the shape over the letters.

The areas of the shape and text that overlap are reversed out.

⑯ Click the Path Selection tool.

⑰ Click the shape and drag it to reposition it in the design if necessary.

The shape interacts differently with the type as it overlaps different areas.

⑱ Click the Background layer to view the design.

#70

DIFFICULTY LEVEL

TIPS

More Options!
You can apply a Layer style to the shapes and letters. Try adding a Bevel and Emboss Layer style. Click Texture and select a pattern for the Texture Elements. The pattern is applied to all the colored areas.

Important!
Whenever you use the Path Selection tool to move letters or the shape, you must target the vector mask layer thumbnail in the Layers palette and click the Exclude Overlapping Shape Areas button on the Options bar to select it.

Did You Know?
You can use the Path Selection tool to move individual letters or the shape separately. Click one letter and move it to create a different look. To undo the move, click the previous state in the History palette.

Chapter 8

Creating Digital Artwork from Photographs

You can use Photoshop to replicate traditional art materials and techniques and see immediate results on your screen. If you have spent years in art school working with traditional materials, you can find a whole new source of creativity as you experiment with different techniques. Even if you have never tried art in any form or claim you cannot even draw a straight line, you can use Photoshop to draw line art, sketch a person or a building, create a painted portrait, or paint with oils and watercolors. You can experiment and try all sorts of projects without wasting any paper products or paints. You can vary colors, mix media, copy, trace, or draw freehand, and even erase the results before anyone else can see your attempts!

The key to creating digital artwork is to combine different layers, effects, smart filters, masks, and blend modes. The results not only vary with the methods used, but also each style of photograph and the subject matter affect the overall look of the finished piece. You can vary methods to make your work more efficient and at the same time expand your creative horizons. With so many options and choices, artistic experimentation with Photoshop can be very addictive. You may spend a lot more time with the art projects than you ever thought you would.

The ten tasks and techniques described in this chapter are only a taste of what is possible.

Top 100

Give any photo
A SKETCHED LOOK

You can make a photo appear to be sketched onto the page, giving a traditional photograph an entirely new look. You can create a title page for an album or a Web gallery or use the technique as the final touch to a painted image. The image appears to be applied to the paper using charcoal, soft pencils, or a paintbrush, leaving the edges and brush marks visible. Starting with any image, you add a new layer filled with white. You then use the Eraser tool to erase through the white to reveal areas of the image

on the underlying layer. Using this technique on a slightly grainy photo even intensifies the effect. You can use any of Photoshop's brushes and change them as you continue sketching the photo onto the page. The greater the number and opacity of the brush strokes, the more of your photograph appears on the white layer. You can vary the style of the strokes by altering the attributes of the eraser from the Brushes palette.

1. Click the Create a New Layer button in the Layers palette.

2. Click Edit.

3. Click Fill.

   The Fill dialog box appears.

4. Click here and select White.

5. Click OK.

A white layer covers the photo.

6. Click the word *Opacity* to activate the scrubby slider and drag to the left just enough to see the image underneath.

7. Click the Eraser tool.

8. Click here.

9. Click a brush with a rough-looking edge.

10. Click and drag the Master Diameter slider to a large brush size.

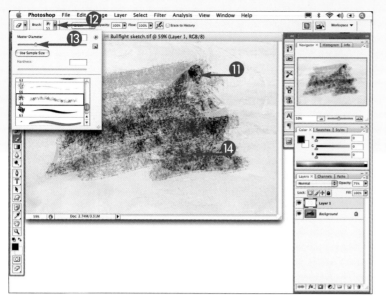

11 Click and drag across the image using several broad strokes.

12 Click here again.

13 Click and drag the Master Diameter slider to a smaller brush size.

14 Click and drag across the image to add more brush strokes.

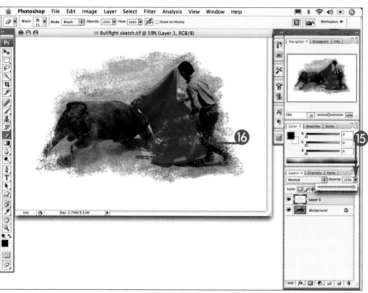

15 Click here and drag the Opacity slider for the layer to 100%.

16 Continue applying just enough strokes until the image looks sketched-in.

The image appears to be brushed or sketched on a page.

More Options!

You can add more brushes to the Brush Preset picker. Click the Brush drop-down arrow in the Options bar to open the Brush Preset picker. Click the arrow to open the Brush Picker menu. Click a brush set from the bottom section, such as Dry Media Brushes. Click Append in the dialog box that appears to add the brushes to the existing list.

Customize It!

You can view brushes by name instead of the stroke thumbnail. Click the Brush drop-down arrow in the Options bar to open the Brush Preset picker. Click the arrow to open the Brush Picker menu. Click Small List or Large List. You can return to the default brush set by selecting Reset Brushes from the same list.

ADD YOUR OWN SIGNATURE
to any artwork

Fine art prints may or may not have a copyright mark; however, they are almost always signed by the artist. You can sign your digital projects one at a time after they are printed, or you can apply a digital signature from within Photoshop. You can create a large custom signature brush and save it in your brushes palette. You can then quickly apply your signature digitally to all your projects.

You can change the Diameter slider in the Brush options and sign your images with any size brush, and you can sign your photo with a color by selecting that color as the foreground color before signing.

You should sign your projects on a separate layer to preserve the layer transparency. You can then add layer styles and easily change the color of the signature or even create a blind embossed signature effect.

Because signing your name with a mouse can be difficult, creating your own signature brush is best accomplished using a Wacom pen tablet as described in Task #10.

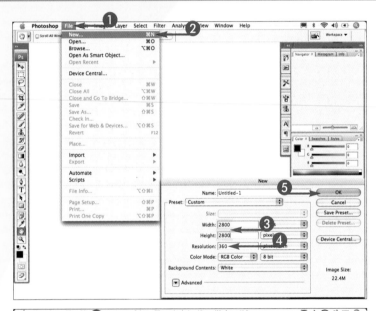

① Click File.

② Click New.

The New dialog box appears.

③ Click in the fields for the size and width and type **2800**.

④ Click in the field for the resolution and type **360**.

Note: Make sure that Background Contents is set to White, the default.

⑤ Click OK.

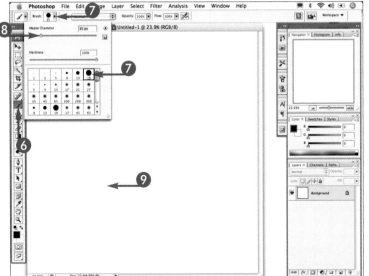

A new blank document appears.

⑥ Click the Brush tool.

⑦ Click here and select a hard-edged brush.

⑧ Click and drag the Diameter slider to make the brush 35 to 40 pixels.

Note: You can pick any hard-edged brush for your signature. The numbers here are just guidelines.

⑨ Click in the blank layer and sign your name.

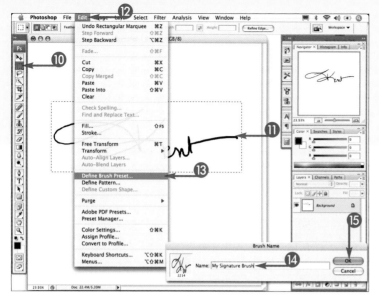

Your signature appears on the white image.

⑩ Click the Rectangular Marquee tool.

⑪ Click and drag just around your signature.

⑫ Click Edit.

⑬ Click Define Brush Preset.

The Brush Name dialog box appears.

⑭ Type a name for your signature, such as **My Signature Brush**.

⑮ Click OK to save the signature brush.

⑯ Open another image to which to add the signature.

⑰ Click here to add a blank layer.

⑱ Click the Brush tool.

⑲ Click here and select your signature brush and click and drag the Master Diameter slider to adjust the size to fit the image.

⑳ Click in the image.

Your signature appears.

● Optionally, you can click the Layer Styles button to add a drop shadow or bevel.

TIPS

Did You Know?

You can create a custom brush from any image or signature up to 2500 by 2500 pixels in size. Signature brushes work best if they are created with a brush with the hardness set at 100%.

Attention!

If you create your original signature in color, the custom brush will still be created in grayscale. You can change the signature color before applying the signature brush to an image or after it is applied on a separate layer.

More Options!

If you add a drop shadow and bevel to the signature layer using the Layer Styles dialog box, you can lower the Fill opacity of the layer to zero to give your signature a blind embossed look.

Create a digital
PEN-AND-INK DRAWING

You can create the look of a pen-and-ink drawing from a photograph using a variety of methods in Photoshop. Often the method you use depends on the subject matter of the original. Photoshop includes many filters such as Find Edges, which finds areas of contrast and outlines these; however, the filter applies the colors in the image to the edges. By changing a duplicated layer to a high-contrast grayscale first and then applying the Smart Blur filter in the Edges Only mode, you get a black image with

white lines. You can then invert the image to get black lines on a white background. Depending on the look that you want, you can apply a filter such as Minimum with a 1-pixel radius to thicken the lines.

Often, the artistic effects do not appear strong enough in a large image. If your art project is still too photographic, you can click File and select Revert and then reduce the image size before applying Photoshop filters to achieve artistic-looking results.

1. Press ⌘+J (Ctrl+J) to duplicate the Background layer.

2. Click Image → Adjustments → Black & White.

   The Black and White dialog box appears.

3. Click here and select Infrared.

   ● You can click any of the other Black and White options, depending on your image, to get a high-contrast grayscale.

4. Click OK.

The image turns into a grayscale image.

5. Click Filter → Blur → Smart Blur.

   The Smart Blur dialog box appears.

6. Type **35** in the Radius field and **35** in the Threshold field.

   *Note: The numbers in step **6** are a guide and will vary with the image and the look that you want.*

7. Click here and select High.

8. Click here and select Edge Only.

9. Click OK.

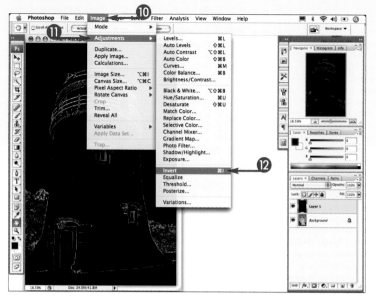

A progress bar appears as the Smart Blur filter is applied, and the image turns black with white outlines.

⑩ Click Image.

⑪ Click Adjustments.

⑫ Click Invert.

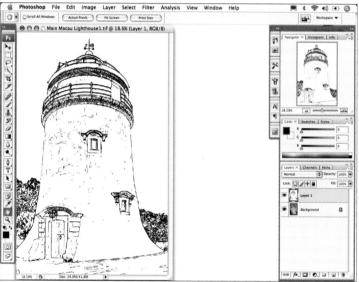

The drawing appears as black lines on a white background.

TIPS

Did You Know?

You can make the lines thicker and darker by clicking Filter → Other → Minimum. Set the Radius to 1 pixel. For heavier lines, try clicking Filter → Artistic → Smudge Stick and reduce the stroke length to 0.

More Options!

You can get better results by increasing the contrast in the original image. After the grayscale conversion, click Image → Adjustments → Levels. Move both sliders slightly toward the center to increase the contrast.

More Options!

You can put the black lines on a separate layer. Click a white area using the Magic Wand tool. Click Select → Similar to select all white areas. Click Select → Inverse. Then press ⌘+J (Ctrl+J).

Give a photograph a
WOODCUT LOOK

A traditional *woodcut* is an engraving made by cutting areas into a block of wood using gouges and knives. The surface is then inked and printed on paper or another material. The uncut areas are raised to receive the ink in a process similar to that of a rubber stamp. A woodcut often has thicker black lines than other types of engravings, depending on the style and skill of the artist. Sometimes the areas that are not inked on the paper show the color of the paper, and other times those areas are painted or

inked as well. You can give a photograph a woodcut look using Photoshop to add a unique creative element to any design. Using a combination of filters and adjustments, you create a grayscale image and turn the grayscale layer into a very high-contrast black and white. Then using the layer blend modes, you allow only the black lines to show through on the background image. By changing the background layer to a smart object, you can change the finished image and customize the settings.

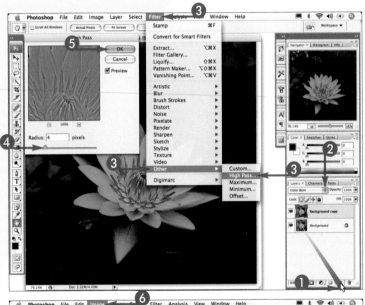

① Click and drag the Background layer over the Create a New Layer button to duplicate it.

② With the top layer selected, click here and select Color Burn.

③ Click Filter → Other → High Pass.

The High Pass dialog box appears.

④ Click and drag the Radius slider until you just start to see the image.

⑤ Click OK.

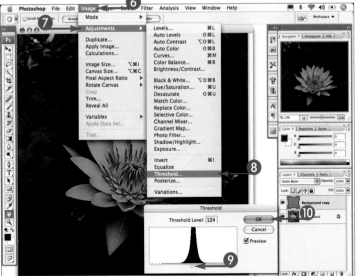

⑥ Click Image.

⑦ Click Adjustments.

⑧ Click Threshold.

The Threshold dialog box appears.

⑨ Click and drag the Threshold Level slider between 123 and 128 to see the outlines of the woodcut.

⑩ Click OK.

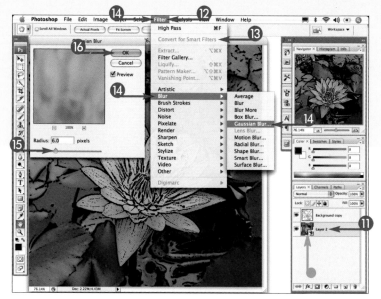

DIFFICULTY LEVEL

⑪ Click the Background layer to select it.

⑫ Click Filter.

⑬ Click Convert for Smart Filters.

● The Background layer icon changes to a smart object icon, indicating that is a smart object.

⑭ Click Filter → Blur → Gaussian Blur.

The Gaussian Blur dialog box appears.

⑮ Click and drag the slider to blur the main image.

⑯ Click OK.

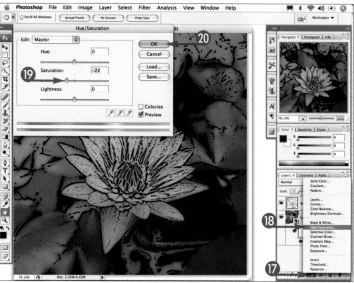

⑰ Click the New Adjustment Layer button in the Layers palette.

⑱ Click Hue/Saturation.

The Hue/Saturation dialog box appears.

⑲ Click and drag the Saturation slider to adjust the look.

⑳ Click OK.

The photo looks like a woodcut with a painted or inked background.

TIPS

Change It!

You can double-click the Hue/Saturation icon to edit the settings. You can double-click the words *Gaussian Blur* in the Layers palette to edit the smart filter and change the amount of blur.

More Options!

The High Pass filter retains edge details wherever there are sharp color contrasts and reduces the rest of the image to a flat grayscale. You can create a woodcut with less detail by lowering the setting of the High Pass filter.

Did You Know?

Setting the threshold below 128 reduces the strength of the woodcut lines. The Threshold command changes images to high-contrast black and white, in which pixels with gray values above 128 turn white and pixels below 128 turn black.

Turn a photo into a
COLORED-PENCIL ILLUSTRATION

Colored-pencil illustrations are found in exhibitions and galleries everywhere. Once thought of as an elementary medium, perfect for children, many artists today are working with colored pencils as a medium in and of itself, and not just for texture studies before using another medium such as watercolor or oils.

You can transform a photograph into a colored-pencil illustration in Photoshop CS3 in many ways, and you will get a more traditional effect by reducing the

image size before you apply the filters. As with most of the Photoshop filters, simply clicking a filter in the Filter Gallery rarely renders the sought-after effect. By simplifying the colors in the image with the Median filter and then applying several filters, the image more closely resembles a traditional colored-pencil drawing. Start by opening the file as a smart object. You can then easily edit the filters after applying them.

① Open the photo as a smart object as in Task #19.

② Press ⌘+J (Ctrl+J) to duplicate the original smart object layer.

③ Click Filter.

④ Click Noise.

⑤ Click Median.

⑥ Click and drag the slider to about 4 to flatten the colors in the image and soften the edges.

   Note: The amount will depend on the image size and the amount of detail in the image.

⑦ Click OK.

⑧ Click Filter → Brush Strokes → Sprayed Strokes.

   The Filter Gallery dialog box appears.

⑨ Click and drag the Stroke Length slider to 20.

⑩ Click here to duplicate the Artistic layer.

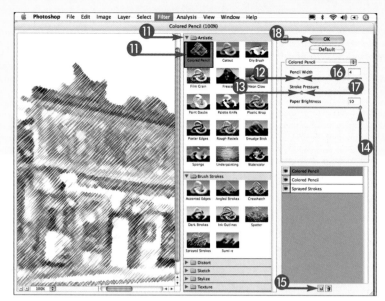

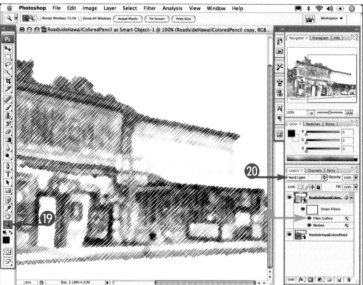

75

DIFFICULTY LEVEL

⑪ Click here and select Colored Pencil for this layer.

⑫ Click and drag the Pencil Width slider to 2.

⑬ Click and drag the Stroke Pressure slider to 15.

⑭ Click and drag the Paper Brightness slider to 50.

⑮ Repeat step **10**.

⑯ Click and drag the Pencil Width slider to 4.

⑰ Click and drag the Stroke Pressure slider to 3.

⑱ Click OK.

The Filter Gallery closes.

⑲ Double-click the Zoom tool to see the drawing at 100 percent.

⑳ Click here and select Hard Light.

The resulting image looks like a colored-pencil drawing.

● You can double-click the Filter Gallery name in the Layers palette to reopen the Filter Gallery and change any settings.

TIPS

Did You Know?

You can turn a colored-pencil illustration into a graphite pencil sketch by clicking the Adjustment Layer button in the Layers palette and clicking Black & White. Change any of the presets to fit your image.

More Options!

To see the document in full on the screen, double-click the Hand tool on the toolbox or click Fit Screen on the Options bar. To zoom to 100 percent, double-click the Zoom tool in the toolbox.

Attention!

Any of the Blend modes in the Lighten and Overlay sections will enhance the colored-pencil sketch. You can also click the bottom layer in the Layers palette and drag the Fill slider to the left for a different look.

POSTERIZE A PHOTO
for a Warhol-style image

Photoshop includes a Posterize command that automatically posterizes an image by mapping the Red, Green, and Blue channels to the number of tonal levels that you set. The Poster Edges filter creates a different look, more like an etching than a posterized print. To create a posterized image more reminiscent of the Andy Warhol style of the 1960s and '70s, you can instead use three adjustment layers in succession. Use a Black and White adjustment layer to convert the photo to a grayscale image. Then apply a Posterize adjustment layer,

specifying the levels that correspond to the number of colors you want in the final image. More levels make the image less stylized as it adds many more colors. Finally, use a Gradient Map adjustment layer to map any color to each of the levels of gray. You can edit any of the adjustment layers to change the colors or levels until you get the look that you want. For the best result, select a photo with a main subject on a plain background or extract the subject and place it on a black background.

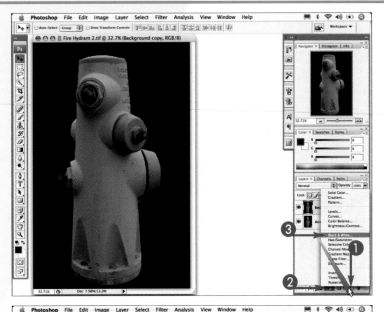

① Click and drag the Background layer over the New Layer button in the Layers palette to duplicate it.

② Click the New Adjustment Layer button to add a new blank layer.

③ Click Black & White.

The Black and White dialog box appears, and the image turns to grayscale.

④ Click Auto to see if the contrast improves.

● Optionally, you can click here and select a preset to enhance the contrast.

⑤ Click OK.

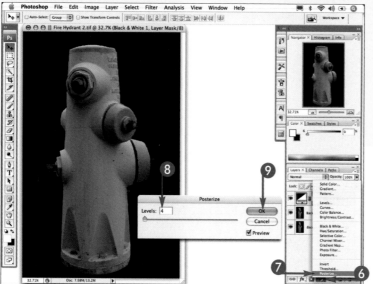

6 Click the New Adjustment Layer button.

7 Click Posterize.

The Posterize dialog box appears.

8 Type **4** in the Levels data field.

9 Click OK.

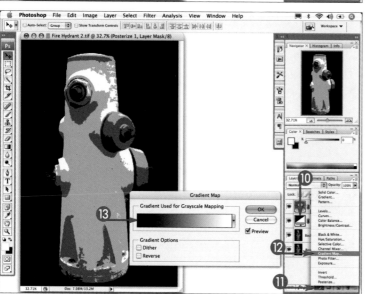

10 Click the Black and White top layer to select it.

11 Click the New Adjustment Layer button.

12 Click Gradient Map.

The Gradient Map dialog box appears.

13 Click in the gradient.

TIPS

Attention!

You get better results if you match the number of gray levels with the number of color stops in the gradient. To add more gray levels, double-click the Posterize thumbnail in the Layers palette and increase the number of levels. Then double-click the Gradient Map thumbnail and add more color stops.

Try This!

If you want a more realistically colored image, fill the color stops on the right in the Gradient Editor with the lightest colors that you want in the image and the color stops on the left with the darkest colors. The greater the number of color stops and the more colors you use, the wilder the image appears.

POSTERIZE A PHOTO
for a Warhol-style image

After posterizing the first photo as in the steps, you can create multiple copies of the posterized image using different colors. Click File → Save As to give this version another name. Save the image in a new separate folder. Click the Gradient Map thumbnail in the Layers palette to open the dialog box again.

Click in the gradient to open the Gradient Editor. Change the colors for each of the four color stops, each time selecting the darkest colors for the leftmost color stops and the lightest colors for the

rightmost color stops. Click OK to close the Gradient Editor and again to close the Gradient Map dialog box. Click Save As and give this second color version another name. Repeat this process until you have four different versions of the image.

To finish the project, create a new blank document and click File → Place to place each of the four images on the page. You can even flip any of the images horizontally to add more variety by clicking Edit → Transform → Flip Horizontal.

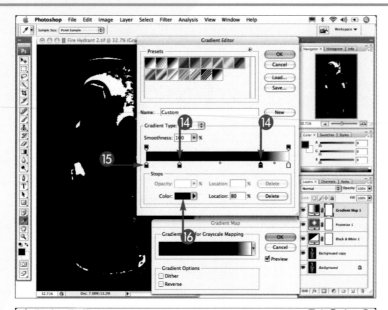

The Gradient Editor appears.

⑭ Click two areas below the gradient bar to add two more color stops.

Note: The number of color stops should match the levels of posterization that you entered.

⑮ Click the leftmost color stop to select it.

⑯ Click the Color thumbnail.

The Color Picker for selecting the stop color appears.

⑰ Click and drag the color slider.

⑱ Click to select the darkest of the four colors you will use.

Note: If the Warning triangle appears, the color is out of gamut for printing and will not print as you see it. Click the small square below the warning triangle to select the closest in-gamut or printable color.

⑲ Click OK.

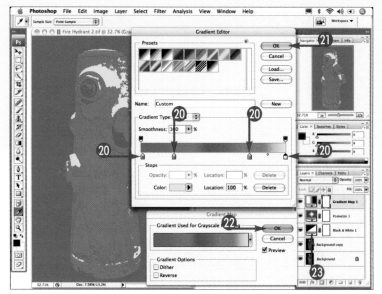

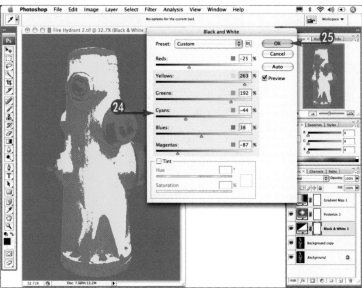

20 Repeat steps **15** to **19**, selecting each of the other three color stops to change the color.

21 Click OK to close the Gradient Editor.

22 Click OK to close the Gradient Map dialog box.

23 Double-click the Black and White adjustment layer thumbnail.

 # 76 CONTINUED

The Black and White dialog box appears.

24 Click and drag the color sliders to adjust the areas of color.

25 Click OK.

The image looks like a posterized and stylized print design from another era.

TIPS

Customize It!

Use the Dodge and Burn tools to change individual areas. Click the Background copy layer and click the Dodge tool. Click and drag in the image to make some areas lighter. Click the Burn tool and click and drag other areas to make them darker. You can lower the Exposure setting in the Options bar to lessen the change.

More Options!

Instead of using a Gradient Map, you can merge the Background copy with the Black and White and the Posterize adjustment layers. Then add colors individually to gray areas. Select the first gray area using the Magic Wand with a tolerance of 0. Click the foreground color and select a new color. Press Option+Delete (Alt+Backspace) to fill the selection.

CREATE A PEN-AND-COLORED-WASH
drawing from a photograph

You can easily transform a photograph into a pen-line-and-colored-wash drawing by applying different filters and adjustments to multiple layers. Because the effect is more pronounced on a simplified and lower-resolution image, start by reducing the image size by setting one of the pixel dimensions in the Image Size dialog box to 1000 pixels. You should brush over the lines and vary the brush opacity as you paint rather than filling in areas with the same opacity. Also start with large brushes and then work

with smaller, more opaque brushes to define the details. By working on duplicates of the Background layer and inserting a blank white layer between the original Background and the layers above, the original image is never edited until you flatten the layers at the end of the project and save the wash drawing with a new name.

As with every project in Photoshop, there are multiple ways you can achieve a similar effect. Each type of photo also gives you a slightly different effect.

1. Press D to reset the foreground and background colors to the default.

2. Click and drag the Background layer over the New Layer button twice to create two duplicated layers.

3. Click the New Layer button to create a new blank layer.

4. Press ⌘+Delete (Ctrl+Backspace) to fill the blank layer with white.

5. Click and drag the white layer below the two Background copy layers.

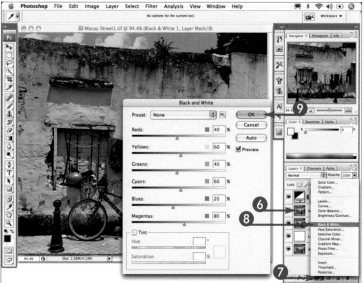

6. Click the Background copy 2 layer to select it.

7. Click the Adjustment Layer button.

8. Click Black & White.

   The Black and White dialog box appears, and the image changes to a grayscale image.

9. Click OK.

174

10 Press ⌘+E (Ctrl+E) to merge the Black and White adjustment layer with the layer below.

11 Click Filter.

12 Click Stylize.

13 Click Find Edges.

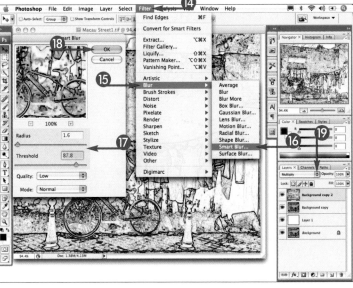

The image changes to resemble a shaded drawing.

14 Click Filter.

15 Click Blur.

16 Click Smart Blur.

The Smart Blur dialog box appears.

17 Click and drag the Radius and Threshold sliders to soften the edges.

18 Click OK.

The amount of detail is reduced. The edges of the lines are softened.

19 Click here and select Multiply for the blend mode.

TIPS

Change It!
Change the brush tip shape before you paint with white on the black mask. With the Brush tool selected, click the Brushes icon to open the brushes palette. Click Brush Tip Shape and change any of the attributes.

Customize it!
You can also create a dual brush to change the brush strokes even more. Click the Brushes icon to open the Brushes palette. Click Dual Brush and click a different brush sample box. Click and drag the sliders to alter the brush style.

More Options!
You can make the drawing appear more traditional by painting with white on the combined Black & White and Find Edges layer. Try this as the last step, after painting in the color on the Background copy layer.

CREATE A PEN-AND-COLORED-WASH
drawing from a photograph

Traditional artists sometimes use India ink and a diluted ink wash to visualize the light and shadow areas before beginning a painting. The technique is also often used in figure studies to create expressive drawings. When applied to a landscape or cityscape, the pen line and diluted ink wash produces an image with a unique look. The drawings are similar to and yet different from traditional watercolors, which generally do not use black lines. In the 17th century,

Nicholas Poussin and Rembrandt applied such techniques to create rich and varied drawings.

You can use this technique to paint with both color or grayscale washes or try tinting the image to a sepia brown after duplicating the Background layer the first time. Apply the Black and White adjustment layer, click the Tint box, and select a tint color using the sliders. Then duplicate the sepia-colored layer, apply the filters, and paint in the washes for a toned drawing.

The colored photo shows through the line drawing.

⑳ Click the Background copy layer to select it.

㉑ Click Filter.

㉒ Click Noise.

㉓ Click Median.

The Median dialog box appears.

㉔ Click and drag the Radius slider to blur the image and colors.

㉕ Click OK.

㉖ Press Option (Alt) and click here to add a black layer mask to the Background copy layer.

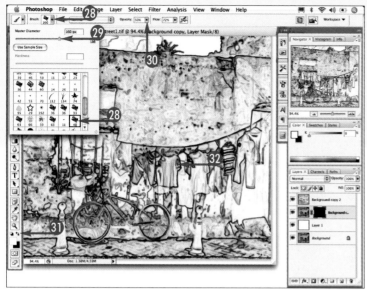

The black mask hides the colored Background copy layer.

㉗ Click the Brush tool.

㉘ Click here and select a large ragged-edge brush.

㉙ Click and drag the slider to increase the brush size if necessary.

㉚ Click here and reduce the brush opacity to 50%.

㉛ Click here if necessary to make sure that the foreground color is white.

㉜ Click and drag in the image painting with white on the mask to bring in the colored wash.

The colors begin to appear in the drawing as large washes.

㉝ Click here and reduce the brush size.

㉞ Click and drag in the image to paint over the details and increase the look of the wash.

Note: *Use brush strokes in the direction that fits the objects in the image.*

The colored wash appears on the image.

TIPS

Did You Know?
You can make the drawing appear to have multiple layers of washes by starting with a very low brush opacity in the Options bar for the first set of brush strokes and then increasing the opacity as you brush a second and third time.

Change It!
Depending on the colors in your photo, you can change the blend mode of the Background copy layer to change the final look of the pen-and-wash drawing. Try Hard Light or Darken for totally different looks.

Attention!
To make the washes appear more traditional, be sure to leave some areas around the edges unpainted, letting the white layer show through to make the drawing appear to be painted on a white piece of paper.

Compose a
PHOTO COLLAGE

Artists and photographers have long been blending separate images into one combined finished piece. Artists may glue disparate items onto a background — hence the word *collage* from the French for gluing. Photographers may combine exposures on one piece of film or combine several images in the darkroom in a *photo montage,* a term taken from the French for mounting or assembling. Photoshop adds many new and easier techniques for creating such artistic composites. Instead of worrying about image registrations or unexpected interactions of shapes

and forms, you can now visually combine multiple images into one by blending pixels. Starting with a basic Photoshop collage technique, you can apply so many variations that the piece can be used for everything from advertising to fine art.

You start with one image as the background and drag other photographs and artwork onto it in separate layers. Then resize and adjust the position of each layer and add masks to blend the images together. Add gradients and paint on the masks, or you can even add masks to masks for more variations.

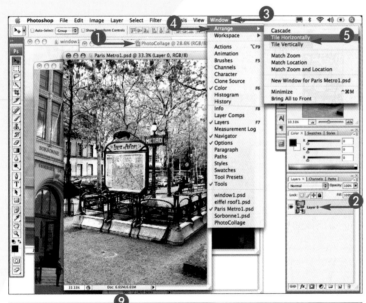

① Create a new blank document the size that you want your collage to be.

② Open each of the images for the collage as a smart object as in Task #19.

③ Click Window.

④ Click Arrange.

⑤ Click Tile Horizontally or Tile Vertically, depending on the size of your monitor so that you can see all the open images at once.

The images are tiled across the screen.

⑥ Click the blank new document and double-click the Hand tool to make it fit the screen.

⑦ Click the Move tool and click and drag the first image onto the blank document.

⑧ Close the first image.

⑨ Click Edit → Free Transform.

⑩ Press Shift and click and drag the corner anchors to size the image.

⑪ Click the Commit button.

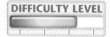

12 Press D to reset the foreground and background colors.

13 Click the Layer Mask button to add a mask to the layer.

14 Click the Gradient tool.

15 Click one of the gradient styles.

16 Click and drag the Gradient tool across the image to blend it with the background.

17 Repeat steps **7** to **16** until all the images are layers in the collage.

18 Click each layer to adjust the placement of the image.

19 Click the layer mask thumbnail and click and drag a different gradient to change the look.

The images blend into one another, creating an artistic photo collage.

TIPS

Important!
Make sure that all your photos for the collage are set to the same color space or convert them to Adobe RGB as you place them. Also check the bit depth and resolution of the images and change these as needed.

Did You Know?
Because you opened each of the images as a smart object, you can safely adjust the size down to fit the image and then change it and make it larger for the final image without losing image quality.

Caution!
The number of additional layers, effects, and layer sets that you can add to an image is limited by your computer's memory. Close any unnecessary files and applications to make as much RAM available as possible for Photoshop to process the collage.

Turn a photo into a
HAND-PAINTED OIL PAINTING

You can use the Filter Gallery and various Photoshop filters to turn any photograph into an image that has a painterly look. However, filters are applied evenly to the active layer of an image and therefore do not appear hand painted. By applying a filter to a layer and then using brush strokes of varied size to paint the filtered image onto a new layer, you can create an oil painting that appears to be painted one stroke at a time. After applying an Artistic filter, you select the total image and define a pattern. Then with the

Pattern Stamp tool and Impressionist option as your paintbrush and the image as the pattern, you brush the image on a new blank layer. You should always start with a large brush and paint in more open areas of the photograph. Reduce the brush size and continue painting in the details. To emphasize a few edges and capture some finer detail, you continue to paint with the Pattern Stamp tool, deselecting the Impressionist option.

① Expand the canvas to create a white border around the photo.

Note: To expand the canvas, use the reverse-crop technique described in Task #23.

A white border appears around the image.

② Click and drag the Background copy layer over the New Layer button to duplicate it.

③ Click Filter.

④ Click Artistic.

⑤ Click Dry Brush.

The Filter Gallery appears with the Dry Brush filter applied in the Preview window.

⑥ Click and drag the sliders to adjust the Dry Brush appearance for your photo.

⑦ Click OK.

The filter is applied to the image.

⑧ Press ⌘+A (Ctrl+A) to select the entire image.

⑨ Click Edit.

⑩ Click Define Pattern.

The Pattern Name dialog box appears.

⑪ Type a new name if you want.

⑫ Click OK.

⑬ Press ⌘+D (Ctrl+D) to deselect the image.

TIPS

Caution!

Take your time to make the image appear hand painted. Change the brush size often. Start with large brushes and make them smaller as you paint in details, deselecting the Impressionist option to emphasize the finest details.

More Options!

If you have a Wacom digitizing tablet, you can choose a larger brush and set the Shape Dynamics option of the brush to Pen Pressure. Press lightly with the stylus to produce small strokes and press harder to produce larger strokes.

Attention!

When you first start painting with a large brush and the Impressionist option selected, click the brush rather than dragging it like a true paintbrush. The effect appears more natural by spreading the paint unevenly.

Turn a photo into a
HAND-PAINTED OIL PAINTING

You can completely cover the layer to create a separate painting or use the newly painted layer in combination with the underlying Dry Brush filtered layer, depending on the look that you want. Toggle the Visibility icon on and off for the Background layers by clicking the eye icon as you work so that you can see the image you are painting.

If you decide to use the top painted layer alone when you have finished painting, you can add a canvas-colored layer as a background to fill in around the edges for a realistic look. Click the New Layer button

in the Layers palette. Drag the new blank layer underneath the top painted layer. Click Edit → Fill. Click the Contents Use arrow and click Color. When the Color Picker appears, select a color for the canvas, such as Red 248, Green 242, and Blue 224. Click OK to close the Color Picker and again to close the Fill dialog box and fill the layer.

Duplicate the top painted layer and apply the Texturizer filter with a canvas texture as a final touch.

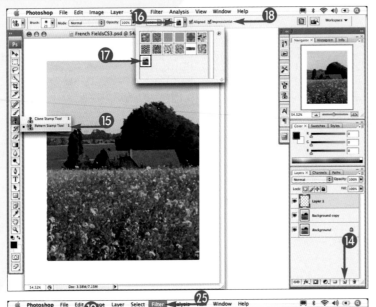

⑭ Click the New Layer button in the Layers palette to add a new blank layer.

⑮ Click the Pattern Stamp tool.

⑯ Click the Pattern thumbnail.

The Pattern Picker opens.

⑰ Click the pattern that you just created of the photo.

⑱ Click Impressionist.

⑲ Click here, select a rough-edged brush, and increase the diameter to fit.

⑳ Click in the layer multiple times to paint the image.

㉑ Repeat steps **19** and **20**, reducing the brush size to paint detailed areas.

㉒ Deselect Impressionist.

㉓ Click to paint and bring back a few photographic details as needed.

㉔ Click and drag the painted layer over the New Layer button.

㉕ Click Filter → Texture→ Texturizer.

The Filter Gallery Texturizer dialog box appears.

26 Click here and select Canvas.

27 Click and drag the sliders to increase the scaling and relief.

Note: The preview image shows the details at 100 percent.

28 Click OK.

The Canvas texture is applied to the finished painting.

Try This!

Click the Pattern Stamp tool and click the Brush thumbnail on the Options bar, opening the Brush Picker presets. Click the drop-down list and click Large List to view the brushes by name. Click the drop-down list again and click Wet Media Brushes. When the dialog box appears, click Append to add the brushes to the current set. Click the brush called Dry Brush on Towel. Open the brush presets by clicking the Brushes palette tab. Click Brush Tip Shape. Click the circular shape and move the dots to change the shape into an oval. Click and drag the arrow in the circle to change the direction to fit your brush stroke style. Paint using your custom brush.

Paint a
DIGITAL WATERCOLOR

Traditional watercolor paintings have transparent colors and loosely defined shapes without black outlines. The surface of the paper often shows through the watercolors to give the image more personality. You can create a digital watercolor from a photograph and make it appear like a traditionally painted image on watercolor paper using a series of filters from the Filter Gallery on separate layers. Start by duplicating the Background layer and applying the first filter. Then duplicate that layer and apply a blur to soften the edges and blend the colors.

Add a blank layer over the other layers, fill it with white, and use it as a background to paint through. Using the eraser set to a chalk-styled brush, vary the opacity and erase through the white layer to reveal parts of the filtered layer below. Finish the painting by merging the two top layers and duplicating the merged layer. Apply a Texture filter to create the watercolor paper look. The final step is to lighten the image by setting the layer blend mode to Screen and brighten the watercolor paints.

① Click and drag the Background layer over the New Layer button to duplicate it.

② Double-click the layer name and type **Dry Brush**.

③ Click Filter.

④ Click Artistic.

⑤ Click Dry Brush.

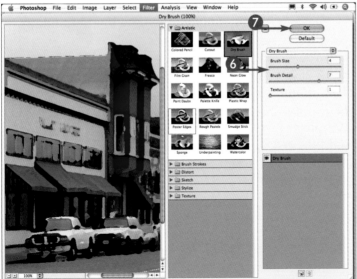

The Filter Gallery appears with the Dry Brush filter applied in the Preview window.

⑥ Click and drag the sliders to adjust the Dry Brush appearance.

⑦ Click OK.

The filter is applied to the image.

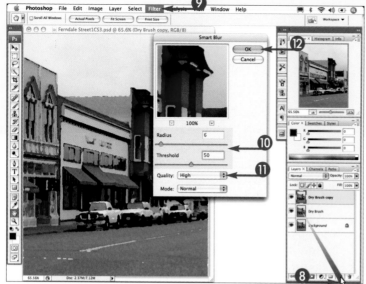

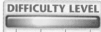

DIFFICULTY LEVEL

⑧ Click and drag the Dry Brush layer over the New Layer button to duplicate it.

⑨ Click Filter → Blur → Smart Blur.

The Smart Blur dialog box appears.

⑩ Click and drag the Radius slider to about 6 and the Threshold slider to about 50.

Note: The numbers are for reference. Your image may require different settings.

⑪ Click here and select High.

⑫ Click OK.

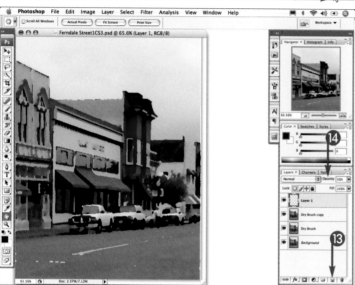

⑬ Click the New Layer button to create a new blank layer.

⑭ Click the word *Opacity* and drag to the left to lower the opacity to 50%.

⑮ Press D to reset the default foreground and background colors.

⑯ Press ⌘+Delete (Ctrl+Backspace) to fill the layer with white.

TIP

Try This!

You can make the paper look more like watercolor paper by using an off-white color to fill the top layer. After creating a new blank layer in step **13**, click Edit → Fill. The Fill dialog box opens. Click the Use arrow and click Color to make the Color Picker appear. Type **250** for the Red data field, **246** for the Green data field, and **239** for the Blue data field to select a color for the watercolor paper. Click OK to close the Color Picker and click OK again to close the Fill dialog box. Erase carefully over just the objects that you want to show as painted on the image. Areas left blank show through as the watercolor paper.

Paint a
DIGITAL WATERCOLOR

Photoshop actually includes a Watercolor filter in the Filter Gallery. This filter generally adds too much black to replicate a traditional watercolor. A true watercolor palette includes only gray and no black paint at all.

Because watercolors not only have soft edges but also minimal transitions of color tones, you get the best results by applying the Reduce Noise or the Median filter to the photo before starting to create the painting. These filters are found in the Filter menu under Noise. By applying a filter first, you

eliminate some of the color changes and sharp edges that make a photograph look like a photograph. With a limited color palette, the Dry Brush filter creates a more painterly image. Then using the Smart Blur filter after the Dry Brush filter has been applied blends the paints to complete the effect.

Traditional watercolor paintings often leave rough edges around the borders and even some blank areas in the painting, so do not completely paint away all the white in the top layer.

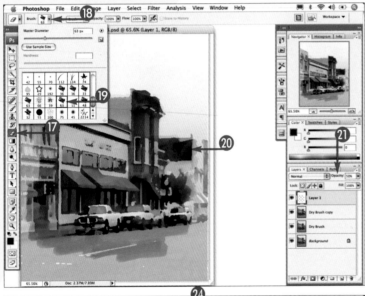

The top layer fills with a translucent white.

⑰ Click the Eraser tool.

⑱ Click the Brush thumbnail.

⑲ Click a large chalk-style brush.

⑳ Click and drag in the document using short strokes until the painting is visible.

㉑ Click the word *Opacity* and drag to the right to increase the opacity to 100%.

㉒ Press ⌘+E (Ctrl+E) to merge the two top layers.

㉓ Click and drag the new merged Dry Brush copy layer over the New Layer button to duplicate it.

㉔ Click Filter.

㉕ Click Texture.

㉖ Click Texturizer.

The Filter Gallery appears with the Texturizer filter.

㉗ Click here and select Sandstone.

㉘ Click and drag the Scaling and Relief sliders to look like rough watercolor paper.

㉙ Click OK.

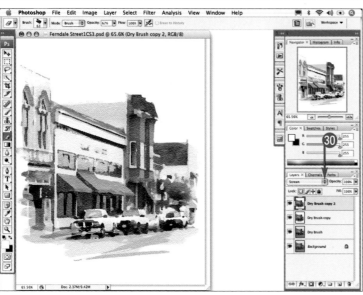

The filter is applied to the top layer.

㉚ Click here and select Screen.

The painting is lightened and looks more like a traditional watercolor.

TIPS

Did You Know?

The paint strokes appear more realistic if you click and drag in the document using short strokes in the same direction as the objects in the image. Paint vertical objects with vertical strokes and horizontal items with horizontal strokes.

Change It!

With the Eraser tool selected, click the Brushes tab to open the Brushes palette. Click the word *Texture* in the brush presets to highlight it. Make changes to the scale, depth, or pattern to add texture to your brush.

Important!

Photoshop's Artistic filters are applied at a fixed size and work best on files smaller than 5MB. Always view your photo at 100 percent to see the effect and wait for the effect to process when changing adjustment sliders.

Chapter

9

Giving Your Images a Professional Presentation

Presentation is so important that even an average photo can appear good when properly displayed or framed. For professional designers, a powerful presentation can help keep an art director happy. For photographers, an elegant display can make all the difference in keeping a client or securing a new one. From the family snapshots to your portfolio, Photoshop makes it easy to show your images in a professional manner.

You can add frames to enhance any image with minimal effort using the one-click frame actions included with Photoshop. You can also create your own frames, change the frame colors and borders, and add a visual matte to the photo. You can create a traditional contact sheet of all the photos in one client folder or on one CD. Using Photoshop's PDF Presentation command, you can easily prepare a custom slideshow with professional transitions, save it as a PDF document, and send it to friends or clients as an email attachment. You can create custom backgrounds to display your images or, for a novel effect, place your images into a traditional slide template. Photoshop can also help you apply an artistic edge to a photo using a sequence of filters from the Filter Gallery, or you can brush an artistic edge onto any images by hand using the Brush tool. You can even use the Picture Package feature to prepare a design layout using different photos for each page. With Photoshop, you can display all your images with a professional touch.

Top 100

Add traditional
PHOTO CORNERS

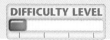

You can add interest and give a finished look to your photographs by adding photo corners to your digital images. You can add these corners easily and quickly using an action from the Actions palette in Photoshop. An *action* is a prerecorded set of commands that are automatically performed in the same sequence when you click the Play button.

Photoshop enables you to record your own actions and also provides a number of predefined actions that are installed with the application. When you first open Photoshop and click the Actions palette tab, you

find a folder called *Default Actions.* In the drop-down list of the Actions palette, there are seven other action folders as well. To create photo corners, you first load the Frames actions and then use the Photo Corners type of frame.

DIFFICULTY LEVEL

Actions are stored as ATN files in the Photoshop Actions folder in the Presets folder.

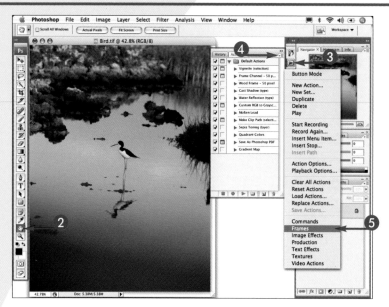

① Open a photo or image.

② Double-click the Hand tool to make the image fit the screen.

③ Click here to open the Actions palette.

④ Click here.

⑤ Click Frames.

The Frames actions are loaded.

⑥ Scroll down to Photo Corners.

⑦ Click Photo Corners.

⑧ Click the Play button.

Photoshop plays the action and places photo corners on the image.

Make a FRAME FROM A PHOTOGRAPH

You may have a photo with more background area than necessary. Rather than crop the photo, you can transform the excess background into a frame for the central focus of the image. Making a frame from the photograph itself is a quick way to give a finished look to any image. You select the area of the photo that you would otherwise crop and then invert the selection to create the frame. You can vary the frame shape by using the Elliptical Marquee tool to create an oval frame. To do so, jump the selected area to

its own layer above the Background layer and change the blend mode to Screen to lighten it.

To separate the frame from the photo even more, you stroke the borders of the new frame layer by applying a layer style. The Layer Style dialog box includes a stroke option with red as the default color; however, you can change it to any color that fits your image. As a final touch, add a drop shadow and an inner shadow, and even a bevel and emboss look.

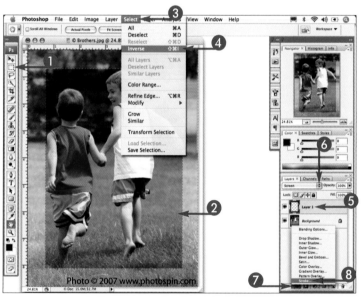

① Click the Rectangular Marquee tool.

② Click and drag a large rectangle in the photo to delineate the frame.

③ Click Select.

④ Click Inverse.

⑤ Press ⌘+J (Ctrl+J) to jump the selection to its own layer.

⑥ Click here and select Screen.

⑦ Click here.

⑧ Click Stroke.

⑨ When the Layer Style dialog box appears, move it to see the image.

⑩ Click the Color thumbnail.

The Color Picker appears.

⑪ Set the color to white and click OK to close the Color Picker.

⑫ Click and drag the Size slider to increase the thickness.

⑬ Click Drop Shadow, Inner Shadow, and Bevel and Emboss.

⑭ Click OK.

The layer style gives the appearance of a realistic frame.

MAKE A CONTACT SHEET
of your photos

Your digital files are like digital negatives. Whether these are photos from a digital camera or scans of traditional prints and negatives, the first file downloaded or scanned is the original. You should always burn a CD or DVD of the originals before you enhance them or use them in projects. Then use the Contact Sheet II feature under Photoshop's Automate command to make a contact sheet to help you identify the images on the CD, DVD, or other storage device. You can also make an index of all the images in one project folder using the same command.

In the Contact Sheet II dialog box, you select the location and the images to be included. You determine the size of the document, the number of rows and columns, and the font and font size for the captions. The size of the thumbnails is constrained by the number of rows and columns. Fewer columns and rows on a page allows for larger thumbnail images. Print the contact sheet on a color printer as a visual index to show a client or for your own reference.

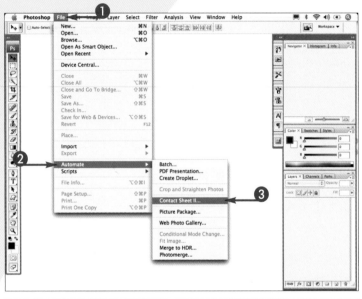

① Click File.

② Click Automate.

③ Click Contact Sheet II.

Note: You can also select the images first in the Bridge and click Tools→ Photoshop → Contact Sheet II.

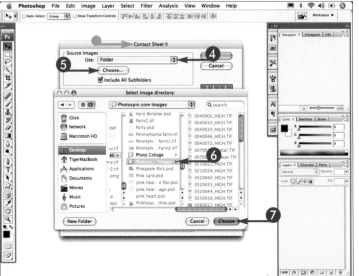

● The Contact Sheet II dialog box appears.

④ Click here and select Folder.

⑤ Click Choose.

A directory dialog box opens.

⑥ Navigate to and click your photo folder.

⑦ Click Choose.

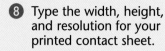

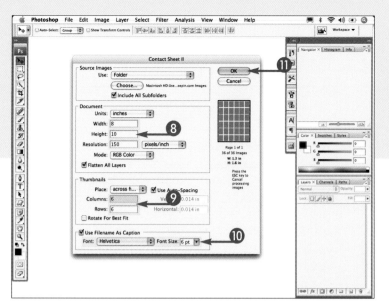

You are returned to the Contact Sheet II dialog box.

⑧ Type the width, height, and resolution for your printed contact sheet.

⑨ Type a number for the columns and rows of thumbnails to be printed.

⑩ Select the font and font size for the printed filename.

⑪ Click OK.

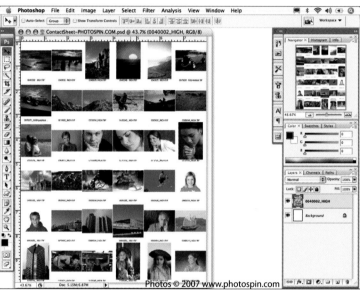

Photos © 2007 www.photospin.com

Photoshop builds and displays your contact sheet.

TIPS

Caution!

The Flatten All Layers command in the Contact Sheet II dialog box flattens the individual photo layers into one so that it prints more quickly. If you deselect the box, Photoshop creates a large, multilayered document and requires large amounts of RAM.

Did You Know?

A document resolution of 150 dpi is sufficient because the thumbnails are so small that the higher resolution would not be a visible improvement. Also, the Contact Sheet II command runs much faster with low-resolution images.

More Options!

To make a contact sheet for a CD/DVD jewel case, type **4.688** inches for both the width and height. Type **5** in each data field for the number of rows and columns. Select 6-point type to fit the text under the thumbnail.

Create a
PDF SLIDESHOW PRESENTATION

If you want to email photos to friends or your portfolio to a prospective employer or send a client some images for review, you can use Photoshop to help you create a slideshow and save it as a PDF presentation. You can then attach the presentation to an email or burn it to a CD or DVD. The PDF Presentation command in Photoshop enables you to combine any type of images into either a multipage document or a slideshow presentation. You determine the image quality depending on where the

presentation will be shown and set a level of security so that the recipient cannot reproduce your images without your permission. You can even select from a number of slide transitions to give your presentation a professional look. You can select a complete folder to use as the source images or use images that are already open. You select the amount of time that each slide appears onscreen and decide if the slideshow should stop after the last image or continue in a loop.

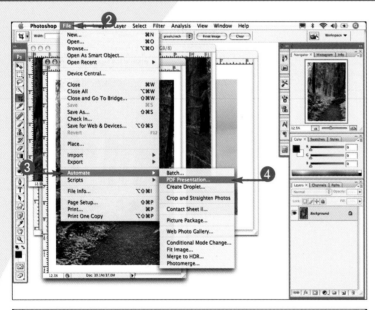

1. Open the images that you want to use for the slideshow.
2. Click File.
3. Click Automate.
4. Click PDF Presentation.

Note: You can also select the images first in the Bridge and click Tools → Photoshop → Contact Sheet II.

The PDF Presentation dialog box appears.

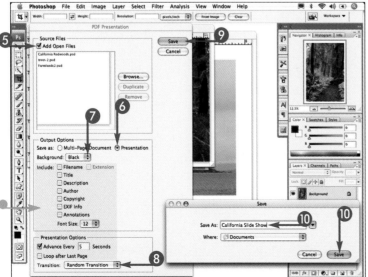

5. Click Add Open Files.

The list of open files appears in the window.

6. Click Presentation.
7. Click here and select a background color.
8. Click here and select a transition style.

● You can click any other attributes for the slideshow that you want.

9. Click Save.

The Save dialog box appears.

10. Type a name for the PDF slideshow and click Save.

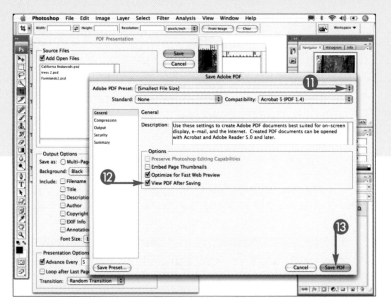

The Save Adobe PDF dialog box appears.

⑪ Click here and select Smallest File Size.

⑫ Click View PDF After Saving.

⑬ Click Save PDF.

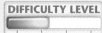

Photoshop creates the PDF file and launches Adobe Reader, Acrobat, or Apple's Preview application, depending on your platform and your default settings.

The PDF slideshow begins in Acrobat, or the individual slides are shown in Preview.

You can press Esc in Acrobat to end the slideshow.

Customize It!

Change the transitions from Random Transition to any of the other transition styles. You can also change how many seconds each image appears on the screen by typing a different number of seconds in the data field under Presentation Options. If you want the presentation to repeat in a continuous loop, click Loop After Last Page.

Attention!

To protect the images from being reproduced without permission, click Security in the Save Adobe PDF dialog box. Click Use a Password in the Permissions section. Type the password in the data field. Set the Printing Allowed and Changes Allowed options to None. Click Save PDF and confirm the password in the dialog box that appears.

Create a
WEB PHOTO GALLERY WITH YOUR COPYRIGHT

In addition to PDF slideshows and contact sheets, you will find other powerful automation tools in Photoshop CS3. Using the Automate command found both under File in Photoshop and under Tools → Photoshop in the Bridge, you can easily create a Web site home page with thumbnail and full-sized images from your files. The Web Photo Gallery command includes a number of templates for gallery styles with various options. You can also include your copyright over each image to help protect your file from being illegally copied when displayed on a Web page.

The steps to creating a Web Photo Gallery are similar to creating a PDF slideshow presentation as shown in Task #84. You select the images, select a style, and add various options such as your contact information, title of the image, and destination for the folder. To add your copyright or any other custom text, you must select the Security options and type the text as you want it to appear on each photo in the gallery.

① In the Bridge, press ⌘+click (Ctrl+click) the images to use in the Web Photo Gallery.

② Click Tools.

③ Click Photoshop.

④ Click Web Photo Gallery.

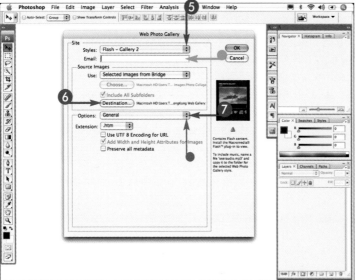

The Web Photo Gallery dialog box appears.

⑤ Click here and select a gallery style.

● You can type a contact email address.

⑥ Click Destination and navigate to and select a folder for the gallery.

⑦ Click here and select Security.

● You can click here and select any of the other options to set various parameters for your Web gallery, including your site name, image size, quality, and image titles.

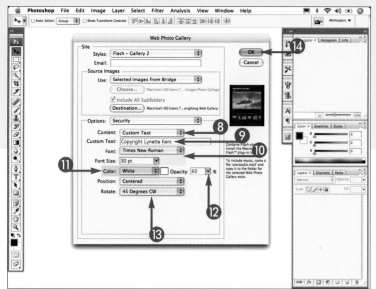

The Security options appear.

⑧ Click here and select Custom Text.

⑨ Click here and type your copyright text.

⑩ Select a font and font size.

85

DIFFICULTY LEVEL

⑪ Click here and select a color.

⑫ Click here and lower the opacity to about 60%.

⑬ Select a position and rotation for the copyright.

⑭ Click OK.

Photoshop automatically resizes the images and creates all the files necessary to upload the gallery to the Web.

Your default browser opens, showing the Web Photo Gallery with your images and copyright.

TIPS

Important!

Before creating the Web Photo Gallery, set the Image Interpolation to Bicubic Sharper — best for reducing image size — in Photoshop's General Preferences. Photoshop automatically uses the interpolation method in the Preferences when resizing source images for the Web Photo Gallery.

More Options!

You can include a banner with each page in the gallery. The banner can include the name of the gallery, the name of the photographer, any contact information, and a date. You can also determine the font and font size in some gallery banner styles.

Try This!

Instead of typing the word *Copyright* as shown in the example here, you can use the copyright symbol. On a Mac, with the Type tool selected, press Option+G before typing your name to add the copyright symbol. On a PC, press Alt+0169 using the numeric keypad.

Give a photo an
ARTISTIC EDGE

You can give any photo a more artistic look by adding an irregular edge using the Filter Gallery and the Brush Strokes filters. By duplicating the Background layer and adding a new blank layer filled with white below the top layer, you can create a unique artistic edge. The Filter Gallery enables you to combine the filters in different ways and use the same technique to create a variety of different edges to fit each different image. Make a selection on the top layer just inside the edge of the photo and then

add a layer mask to delineate the borders of the photo. The artistic edge starts from the selected area. Open the Filter Gallery and start adding different layers of Brush Stroke filters. The Preview window of the Filter Gallery shows the edge effect in reverse. The white areas represent the photo area, and the black areas represent what will be cut away. Every time you change the various sliders for the Brush Stroke filters, your edge effect changes in the Preview window of the Filter Gallery.

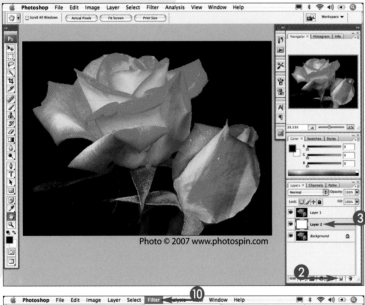

Photo © 2007 www.photospin.com

You can press F three times to view the image in full-screen mode with menus.

1 Press ⌘+J (Ctrl+J) to duplicate the Background layer.

2 Click the New Layer button.

3 Click the new blank layer and drag it between the Background layer and Layer 1.

4 Press D to reset the default colors.

5 Press ⌘+Delete (Ctrl+Backspace) to fill the empty layer with white.

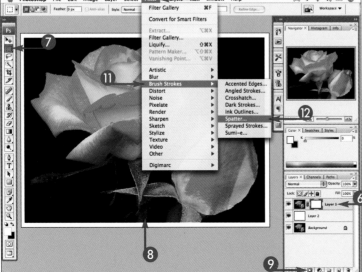

6 Click Layer 1 to target it.

7 Click the Marquee tool.

8 Click and drag a selection just inside the edge of the image.

9 Click the Layer Mask button to add a layer mask to Layer 1.

The image has a small white border.

10 Click Filter.

11 Click Brush Strokes.

12 Click Spatter.

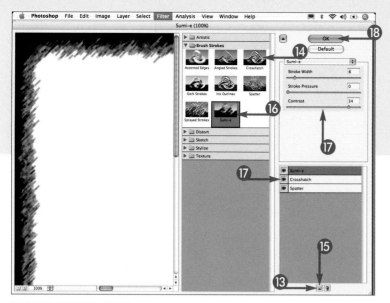

The Filter Gallery opens with the Spatter edge applied.

⑬ Click the New Effect Layer button.

⑭ Click Crosshatch.

⑮ Click the New Effect button again.

⑯ Click Sumi-e.

⑰ Click each individual effect layer and adjust the sliders to get the edge that you want.

⑱ Click OK.

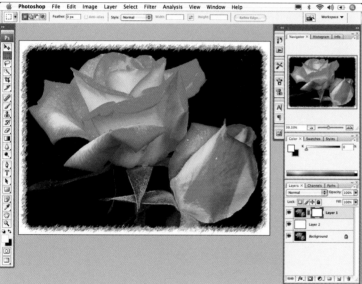

The custom edge is applied to the photo.

TIPS

Did You Know?
Add as many Filter Effects layers as your computer's memory allows. Each one you add changes the style of the effect. Change the order of the layers in the Filter Gallery dialog box, and the overall effect changes as well.

More Options!
For a light-colored image, darken the edge for a stronger effect. Click the Layer Style button in the Layers palette. Click Drop Shadow. Drag the Distance slider to 0. To darken it more, click Inner Shadow also and drag its Distance slider to 0.

Try This!
Click the Layer Style button in the Layers palette. Click Stroke. Click the Color thumbnail and change the default color to black. Click the Position arrow and select Inside. Move the Size slider to get the thickness of line that you want.

Create a
CUSTOM SLIDE TEMPLATE

You can create a template that looks like a traditional photographic slide mount and use it to feature your photos when you print them or even use the photos mounted as slides in a PDF slideshow. After you create the custom slide template, you can use it over and over again with any image.

You can create a slide with any color or use a gray or off-white color similar to a traditional slide mount. You use the Rounded Rectangle tool to create the basic shape and the Rectangular Marquee tool to cut

out the photo viewing area. You apply a drop shadow to give the illusion of a traditional slide mount. Save the template with both a white Background layer and the slide layer so that you can sandwich an image between them for the final slide.

You can add text to the slide, fading it back so that the text looks authentic, and make a slide template customized for each of your clients or friends for a unique presentation.

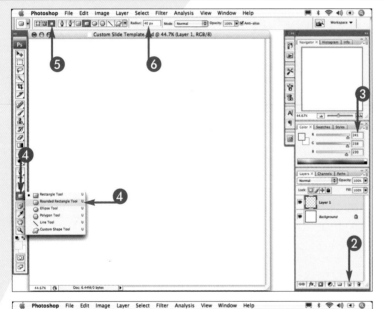

① Create a new file, 5 inches by 5 inches at 300 ppi.

② Click here to add a blank layer.

③ Click the Color palette and type **241**, **238**, and **230** in the data fields for a light-gray color.

④ Click and hold the Rectangle tool and select the Rounded Rectangle.

⑤ Click the Fill Pixels button.

⑥ Type **40 px** in the Radius data field.

⑦ Press Shift and click and drag a square shape in the layer.

⑧ Click the Rectangular Marquee tool.

⑨ Click and drag a rectangular shape in the center of the slide.

⑩ Press Delete (Backspace) to create the hole in the slide.

⑪ Press ⌘+D (Ctrl+D) to deselect.

⑫ Click the Layer Style button.

⑬ Click Drop Shadow.

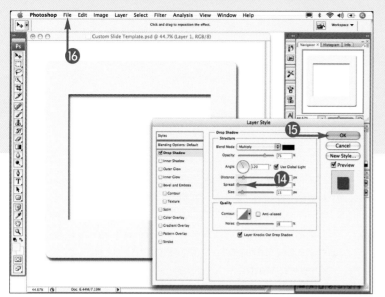

The Layer Style dialog box appears.

⑭ Click and drag the Distance and Size sliders to about 15 to give the slide depth.

⑮ Click OK.

The design resembles a traditional slide mount.

⑯ Click File → Open and open a photo that you want to place in the slide mount.

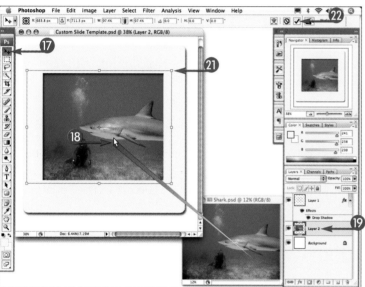

⑰ Click the Move tool.

⑱ Click and drag the photo on top of the slide template.

⑲ Click the photo layer and move it between the other two layers.

⑳ Press ⌘+T (Ctrl+T) to add transformation anchors.

㉑ Press Shift to maintain the aspect ratio of the image as you click and drag the corner anchors to fit it inside the slide.

㉒ Click here to commit the transformation.

The photo appears to be inside a traditional slide mount.

TIPS

Try This!
You can add text to your slide. To do so, click the Type tool and type the text above and below the opening in the center. Use all caps in a font such as Helvetica for a realistic effect. Then lower the opacity of the Type layer to 50%. Press ⌘+E (Ctrl+E) to merge the type layer with the slide layer.

Apply It!
To use your slide on multiple photos, drag the first photo on top of the slide file. Drag the photo layer between the slide and the Background layer. Adjust the photo using the transformation anchors and flatten the layers. Click File → Save As to save the filled slide with a new name. Repeat this process for each of the photos.

Create your own
CUSTOM EDGE

Custom edges add an artistic look to any photograph. You can let a Photoshop filter draw an artistic edge for you as in Task #86, or you can create your own custom edge. Your custom edge can be your personal digital signature. You use the Brush tool on a separate layer and any rough-edged brush. The default brush set that installs with Photoshop includes various rough-edged brushes; however, you can find many more in the brush sets listed in the drop-down list of the Brush Preset Picker.

To create a custom edge, you need to cut the photo out of the Background layer and put it on a separate layer. Then using the Crop tool, you create a reverse crop to enlarge the canvas. Add a transparent layer in between and paint your custom edge on that layer, clicking and dragging around the edges of the photo. Make sure that the black edges extend underneath the photo and paint as much or as little of a visible edge as you want.

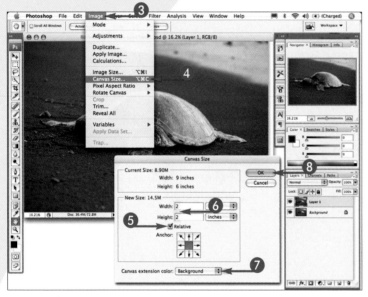

① Press D to reset the foreground and background colors to black and white.

② Press ⌘+J (Ctrl+J) to duplicate the photo layer.

③ Click Image.

④ Click Canvas Size.

   The Canvas Size dialog box appears.

⑤ Click Relative.

⑥ Type **2** in both the Width and Height fields.

⑦ Click here and select Background.

⑧ Click OK.

   A white border appears around the photo.

⑨ Double-click the Hand Tool to fit the image to the screen.

⑩ Press B to select the Brush tool.

⑪ Click here to open the Brush Preset Picker.

⑫ Click here.

⑬ Click Large List.

   The brush presets change to labeled thumbnails.

⑭ Click a rough-edged brush such as Oil Pastel Large.

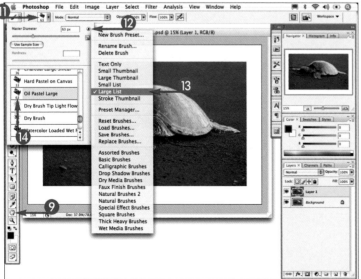

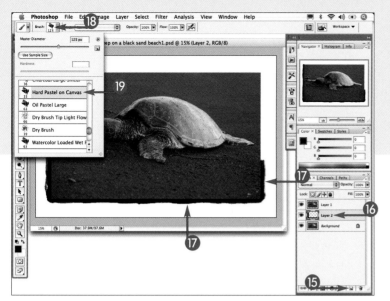

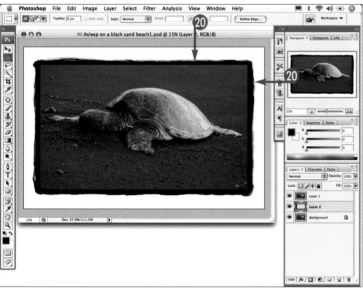

15 Click here to add a new blank layer.

16 Click and drag the blank layer between the other two layers.

17 Click and drag to paint on the blank layer along the visible edge of the photo.

Note: Make sure to paint partially over the edge of the photo.

18 Click the Brush thumbnail.

19 Click another brush such as Hard Pastel on Canvas.

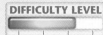
DIFFICULTY LEVEL

20 Continue painting brush strokes around the edge of the photo to add variety to the edge.

The photo appears with a custom border, giving it a unique look.

TIPS

Did You Know?

You can paint with different brush angles for more variety. Click the Brushes tab and click Brush Tip Shape. Click and drag on the Brush Roundness and Angle thumbnail to narrow the circle. Paint the vertical edges of the photo. Click the Brushes tab again and reverse the angle for the brush before painting the horizontal edges.

More Options!

To blend the photo softly into the custom edge, you first click the top photo layer. Use the Rectangular Marquee tool to make a selection just inside the edge of the photo. Click Select → Inverse. Click Select → Modify → Feather. Type **10** in the Feather Radius and click OK. Press Delete to soften the edge of the photo and blend it into the custom border.

Make one photo look like
MANY COMBINED SNAPSHOTS

You can combine multiple photos into one larger file as separate layers, adding borders and drop shadows to create an advertising piece or just a unique image. However, you can easily achieve a similar effect from just one photograph. Start by selecting different sections of the photo and making separate layers of the selections. Then add the same layer style to each layer to make the one photograph appear to be a combination of separate photos pieced together.

You can use this technique on a photograph with many subjects, as for a group shot or a party photo. You can also divide one main subject into various parts. You can vary the size and shape of the individual selections or keep them all the same. You can rotate the individual selections or rotate the individual layers for a completely different effect. You can even apply different colored photo filters to individual layers to change the mood of the photograph.

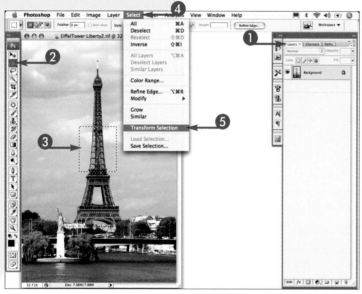

① Arrange the workspace so that the Layers palette is large.

Note: See Task #3 for details.

② Click the Rectangular Marquee tool.

③ Click and drag a rectangle in the image.

④ Click Select.

⑤ Click Transform Selection.

Note: Pressing ⌘+T (Ctrl+T) also adds transformation anchors; however, these transform or rotate the image inside the selection.

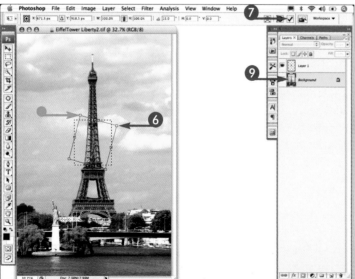

● Transformation anchors appear on the selection border.

⑥ Click and drag just outside a corner anchor to rotate the selection border.

⑦ Click here to apply the transformation.

⑧ Press ⌘+J (Ctrl+J) to duplicate the selection to a separate layer.

⑨ Click the Background layer to select it.

⑩ Repeat steps **3** to **9** to make any number of separate layers.

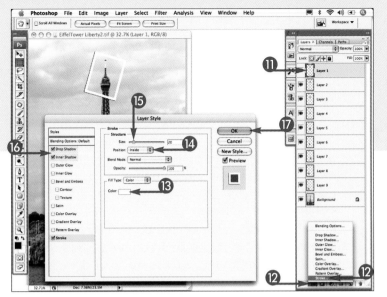

The image appears the same but with multiple layers.

⑪ Click the top layer.

⑫ Click here and select Stroke.

89

The Layer Style dialog box appears.

⑬ Click here to open the Stroke Color dialog box, click white, and press Return (Enter).

⑭ Click here and select Inside.

⑮ Click and drag the Size slider to make the edge larger.

⑯ Click Drop Shadow and Inner Shadow.

⑰ Click OK.

The layer styles are applied to the top layer.

⑱ Press Option (Alt) and click here and drag the layer styles to the layer below.

⑲ Repeat step **18** for each layer.

The final image appears to be a combination of many smaller photos.

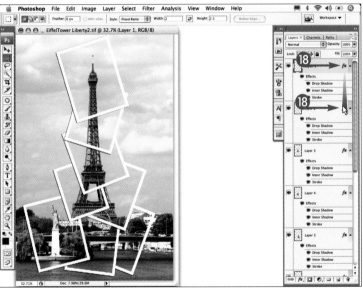

TIPS

More Options!

Depending on your image, you can also rotate the individual layers to make each snapshot's subject appear to be angled. After duplicating the selection to its own layer, press ⌘+T (Ctrl+T) to bring up the transformation anchors. Click and drag just outside an anchor and rotate the layer for a very different effect.

Try This!

Add different colored filters to some or all of the snapshot layers. Click a layer in the Layers palette to select it. Click Image → Adjustments → Photo Filter. Click the Filter arrow to select a color and click OK. Be sure to use the Photo Filter option found under Image Adjustments and not a photo filter adjustment layer because adjustment layers affect all the layers below it.

Make a photo look like a
GALLERY PRINT

You can give your photograph a professional finish by making it look like a gallery print. Gallery prints generally have wide white, black, or even gray borders. The photo is placed in the top portion of the border or frame area, allowing for the name of the gallery, name of the artist, and the name of the artwork to fit under the image in stylized type. You can make a gallery print using either a color or a grayscale photograph. After making a selection of the

photo and cutting it out onto its own layer, you enlarge the canvas size by 3 inches all around the photo. You then add another inch below the photograph, extending the area for the text. Adding a stroke around the photo and a second stroke just into the extended canvas gives a finished look to the gallery print. The strokes can be the same or different colors and pixel width.

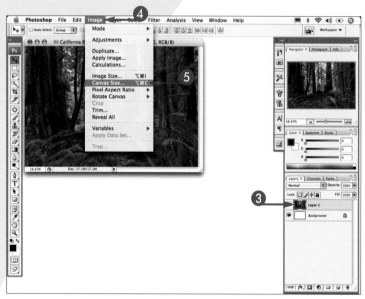

① Press D to reset the foreground and background colors to white and black.

② Press ⌘+A (Ctrl+A) to select the photo.

③ Press ⌘+Shift+J (Ctrl+Shift+J) to cut the photo out of the background and jump it onto its own layer.

④ Click Image.

⑤ Click Canvas Size.

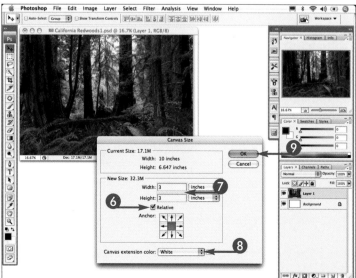

The Canvas Size dialog box appears.

⑥ Click Relative.

⑦ Type **3** in both the Width and Height data fields to add 3 inches to the canvas in each direction.

⑧ Click here and select White.

⑨ Click OK.

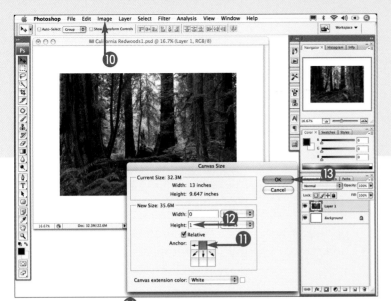

The image is centered in a wide white border. #

Click Image → Canvas Size to open the Canvas Size dialog box again.

⑪ Click the top-center square of the Anchor grid.

⑫ Click in the Height data field and type **1** to add 1 inch to the bottom of the white border.

⑬ Click OK.

90

DIFFICULTY LEVEL

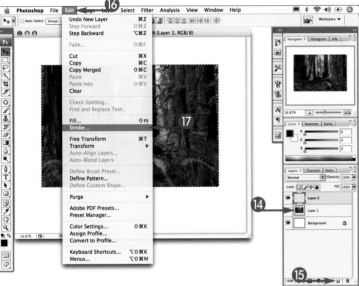

The photo is offset in the white border.

⑭ Press ⌘+click (Ctrl+click) the photo thumbnail to select the photo.

⑮ Click the New Layer button to add a new blank layer.

⑯ Click Edit.

⑰ Click Stroke.

Try This!
Give the title text a true gallery look by using all capital letters and wide tracking. Click the Character button in the palette dock to open the Character palette. Increase the tracking for the title text to separate the letters.

More Options!
For a realistic look, type a print number or the words **artist's proof** on the left side under the border. You can make the stylized letters appear to be written in pencil by lowering the opacity of the Type layer.

Change It!
Set the canvas color to black in the Canvas Size dialog box for a dramatic effect. Use white for the inside border stroke color and gray for the outside border stroke color and type the text using white or gray.

Make a photo look like a
GALLERY PRINT

By placing the strokes on separate layers, you can adjust the opacity of the stroke to change the look of the gallery print. Select the photo on the layer thumbnail to target it and add an empty layer. Using the selection and targeting the new layer, add a stroke around the photo to make it stand out. Still using the same selection, transform the selection to make it slightly wider and higher. Then add another empty layer to add another stroke just outside the first one.

Gallery prints often have the name of the gallery set in a serif-styled font in all capital letters. Widen the tracking of the letters to increase the space between the letters to add a realistic look. You can also use this space to type your name, your studio, or even the name of the image. Select a script font to sign your work under the outside stroke and add a print number to complete the gallery print look.

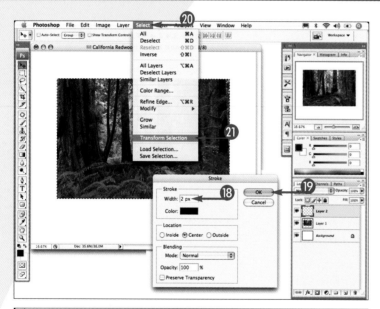

The Stroke dialog box appears.

⑱ Type **2 px** in the Width data field.

⑲ Click OK.

A thin, black stroke is applied to the image.

⑳ Click Select.

㉑ Click Transform Selection.

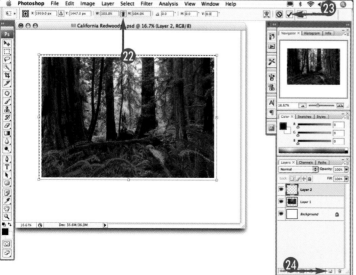

Anchor points are added to the selection.

㉒ Type **103.0%** in the W data field and **104.0%** in the H data field.

㉓ Click here to commit the transformation.

㉔ Click the New Layer button.

㉕ Repeat steps **16** to **19** to add a black stroke outside the border of the photo.

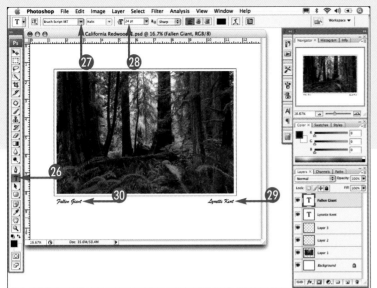

26 Click the Type tool.

27 Click here and select a font that looks like handwriting.

28 Type a font size in the data field.

29 Click here, type your name, and press Enter (Ctrl+Enter).

30 Click here, type a name for the image, and press Enter (Ctrl+Enter).

90 CONTINUED

31 Click in the center of the gallery frame and type the name of the photo studio, gallery, or print series.

32 Press Enter (Ctrl+Enter).

33 Click here and select a serif font such as Adobe Garamond and a font style such as Regular.

34 Type a font size in the data field.

35 Press Enter (Ctrl+Enter) to commit the font changes.

The image now appears like a traditional gallery print.

TIP

More Options!

The size of the stroke that you apply to the borders depends on the size and resolution of the image. Use a thicker stroke for both the border of the photo and the outside border if the image is large or if you want to give the photo more of a framed look. You can also use different colors for the stroke for different effects. If the photo is light in color, try using a shade of gray to stroke the inner border instead of black. Because each stroke border is on its own layer, you can also lower the opacity of the layer if the color of the stroke appears too bold.

Plugging into Photoshop CS3

Although Photoshop CS3 includes a variety of different brushes, shapes, and filters and comes with the Bridge application for organizing and viewing images, third-party plug-ins can help you improve your images more easily and often offer more functionality than Photoshop alone.

Plug-ins exist for nearly every project and for every user level. With the imaginative brush sets, frames, backgrounds, ornaments, and edges from Graphic Authority, you can quickly enhance or totally change the look of your photos. Andromeda's many filters enable you to make a variety of changes to a photograph, including turning a photo into an engraving while controlling every line and direction. Alien Skin not only makes plug-ins for creating glass, chrome, and perspective shadows, but also the BlowUp plug-in, which enables you to resize images while maintaining the highest

image quality. Alien Skin's new Snap Art helps you quickly turn any image into traditional-looking art. Akvis Coloriage enables you to accurately colorize black-and-white photos. Vertus Fluid Mask, the most powerful masking tool ever designed, helps you easily make difficult selections. Using Nik Software's Sharpener Pro and Dfine to sharpen and reduce noise removes the guesswork from Photoshop's filters. Nik Software's Color Efex Pro provides the ultimate control over your colors and makes it easy to create professional-looking images. Extensis Portfolio 8 can help you organize, categorize, archive, and find your digital images from the time you first upload them to the computer through storing them on external media.

Third-party plug-ins can enhance the way everyone uses Photoshop.

Top 100

Embellish a photo effortlessly with
GRAPHIC AUTHORITY
frames and photo ornaments

You can easily add a custom edge and background to give any photograph a professional or artistic style using any one or a combination of Graphic Authority's collections. Graphic Authority offers brushes, backgrounds, papers, album layouts, templates, ornaments, edges, and frames, which work with any version of Photoshop. You can make your photographs look like filmstrips or create an almost unlimited variety of composite images. You can age a photo with backgrounds and brushes or apply a specially designed custom shape to add personality to any

image. Because Graphic Authority's backgrounds, edges, and frames are multilayered Photoshop files, you can easily and completely alter the look of your photo by turning off the visibility of any of the layers.

You can also customize any of Graphic Authority's products to fit your image by transforming edges with the Free Transform command or by adding layer styles and colored filters to various layers to turn any photo into a unique and artistic piece.

At graphicauthority.com, you will find a variety of imaginative products and tutorials.

Photo © 2007 www.photospin.com

① Open a Graphic Authority frame and the photo file.

② Click the Move tool.

③ Click and drag the photo onto the frame image.

Note: *You can open or place the photo as a smart object to preserve the image's source content.*

④ Click and drag the photo layer below the Your Image Here layer.

⑤ Close the photo file.

⑥ Click here to hide the Your Image Here layer.

● You can click the Visibility icon to hide any other layer to alter the look.

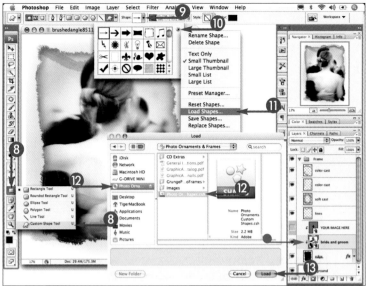

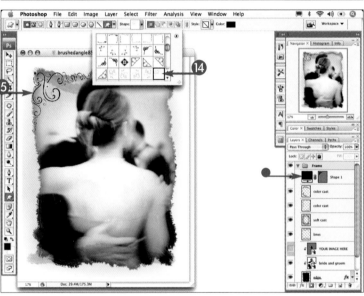

- The photo appears recessed in the Layers palette.

⑦ Use the Move tool to adjust the photo in the frame.

⑧ Click the Custom Shape tool.

⑨ Click here.

⑩ Click here.

⑪ Click Load Shapes.

⑫ When the Load dialog box appears, navigate to the Photo Ornaments CD and click the Photo Ornaments.csh file.

⑬ Click Load.

The Graphic Authority photo ornaments now appear in the Custom Shape Presets.

⑭ Click a Custom shape.

⑮ Click and drag in the photo frame file to add the ornament.

- You can click here for the Shape layer and change the color of the ornament to match a color in the image.

The photo is now framed with an ornamental edge.

91

DIFFICULTY LEVEL

TIPS

Did You Know?

With Graphic Authority products, you will not have to pay to upgrade a plug-in when you upgrade your version of Photoshop. Graphic Authority's backgrounds, edges, and frames are multilayered Photoshop files and can be used with any version of Photoshop. The brushes and ornaments can be loaded into any version of Photoshop CS.

Try This!

You can adjust the edges layer even with the clipping mask applied. Click the edge layer and press ⌘+T (Ctrl+T) to bring up the transformation anchors. Press ⌘+0 (Ctrl+0) to see the anchors if necessary. Click and drag the anchor points until the edges look the way you want.

MAKE A DIGITAL ENGRAVING
with Andromeda's Screens filter

Andromeda Software makes a number of Photoshop plug-ins to help you create a variety of high-quality engraved, etched, or screened effects from any image quickly and easily. Andromeda's filters do all the work. Using Andromeda's Screens plug-in on a grayscale photo, you can select from a variety of different line art screens to turn your photo into a mezzotint or other form of line art. You can select a screening preset from a varied menu. Then using the Threshold slider, you can increase or decrease the amount from fine to coarse. You can select the

number of lines per inch and view a continuous update in a Preview window. You can even apply the effects to the entire image or just to a selection. You can also duplicate the Background layer of a colored image, change the duplicate layer to a grayscale image, and apply the Screens filter to the duplicated layer. You can then get a totally different result by setting the layer blend mode to Overlay. The color from the original image in the layer underneath shows through for a unique effect.

① Click and drag the Background layer over the New Layer button to duplicate it.

② If you are using a color image, convert the duplicated layer to a grayscale image as in Task #49.

③ Click Filter.

④ Click Andromeda.

⑤ Click Screens.

The Screens dialog box appears.

⑥ Click Sync to match the Input and Output image windows.

⑦ Press ⌘+click (Ctrl+Click) and drag in the Preview window to move the thumbnail box.

⑧ Hover the mouse over the Preview window and click to magnify the views.

⑨ Click here.

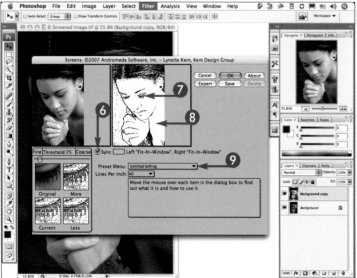

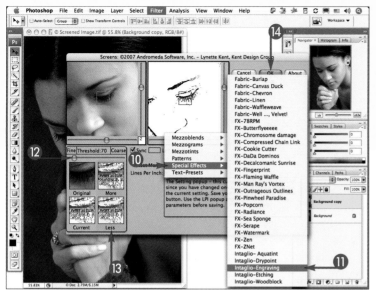

DIFFICULTY LEVEL

⑩ Click a Screens style.

⑪ Click a subset style.

The preview changes.

⑫ Click and drag the Threshold slider to make the lines finer or more coarse.

⑬ Click in the More or Less boxes to increase or decrease the effect.

⑭ Click OK.

The Screens filter applies an engraved look to the image.

● You can click here and select Overlay to make the color image appear through the engraving, changing the look of the final image.

TIPS

Did You Know?

Clicking Expert changes the Screens dialog box and opens more controls. You can increase the amount of unsharp mask to enhance the final results. You can select how the patterns and screens interact. Selecting the Sync option enables you to preview the same areas in the thumbnails of the Input and Output images as you zoom.

Try This!

Click the More or Less thumbnails for the threshold in the filter to increase or reduce the darkness of the lines. If the Threshold slider is set to Fine, clicking the thumbnails changes the threshold by lower amounts each time that you click. Setting the Threshold slider to Coarse causes the changes to vary by greater numbers with each click.

ENLARGE IMAGES
with maximum quality with Alien Skin BlowUp

When you change the image size in Photoshop, you select an interpolation method such as Bicubic Smoother or Bicubic Sharper for resampling the pixels. Although Photoshop's algorithms are good, resampled images lose image quality, most noticeably when enlarged. Alien Skin's BlowUp plug-in enlarges images using a different, more advanced interpolation method. You can use BlowUp to enlarge your photos while preserving the highest quality in your image and avoiding the stairstep, or halo, and fringe artifacts that appear with other enlargements.

You can enlarge 8-, 16-, and 32-bit RGB images as well as CMYK files, making this plug-in perfect for amateur and professional photographers as well as graphic designers.

Alien Skin's BlowUp is an automation tool. Because most of the resizing controls in BlowUp look just like Photoshop's Image Size dialog box, using BlowUp is very easy. In addition, not only does BlowUp let you automatically create a duplicate of the image before resizing, but it also adds more power and control with the photo grain and sharpening controls.

① Open the photo to enlarge.

② Click File.

③ Click Automate.

④ Click Alien Skin Blow Up.

The Alien Skin Blow Up dialog box appears, showing the current dimensions and image size.

⑤ Click the red box and drag over the main subject.

⑥ Click here to constrain the proportions of the original image.

⑦ Click here to resize a copy of the image, leaving the original file untouched.

⑧ Click in the Width data field and type the width that you want.

⑨ Click in the Resolution data field and type the resolution that you want.

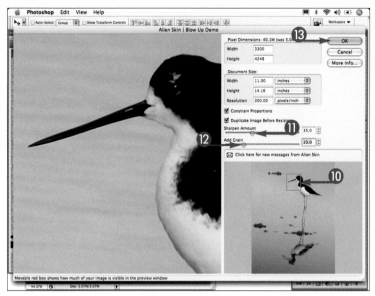

A progress bar on the bottom appears briefly, and the large preview image displays the results.

⑩ Click and drag the red box over the main subject.

⑪ Click and drag the Sharpen Amount slider while watching the large preview to sharpen any softened edges.

⑫ Click and drag the Add Grain slider to reduce any artificial smoothness.

⑬ Click OK.

BlowUp enlarges a duplicate of the image and assigns the same name as the original but with the word *copy*.

TIPS

Did You Know?

Enlarging images always softens edges. Alien Skin's BlowUp includes a Sharpen Amount slider for the most effective method of sharpening an enlarged image and does not create additional artifacts.

Attention!

BlowUp's Sharpen slider only sharpens edges when a photo has been enlarged. Use Photoshop's Sharpen filters to sharpen the original image before enlarging. Always use BlowUp's Sharpen Amount slider carefully to avoid making the photo appear too smooth.

More Options!

You can use BlowUp's Add Grain slider to visually restore overly smooth details by applying artificial film grain. For extreme enlargements, however, you may need to use a more powerful tool, such as Alien Skin's Exposure to add the correct amount of grain.

CHANGE YOUR PHOTO INTO ART
with Alien Skin Snap Art

Turning a photograph into a fine art piece such as an oil painting or a pencil sketch using Photoshop's actions and brushes can be a lot of fun. It can also be time-consuming. You can instead use Alien Skin Software's new Snap Art plug-in to transform photos into natural media art with just a few clicks. You can start with the factory settings to make your photo appear hand-painted or drawn or change any setting to create your own effects.

The Snap Art dialog box includes a large Preview window and even several split screen previews so that you can see the effects on your photo as you apply them. Many of the settings include texture and lighting controls to give your project the look of realistic art. You can experiment with Snap Art for almost limitless variations. You can even combine effects on separate layers for a completely different art style.

You will find many other powerful plug-ins at www.alienskin.com.

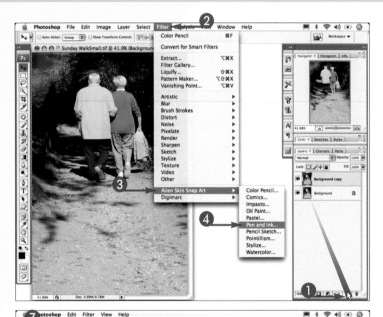

CREATE A PEN-AND-INK DRAWING

① Click and drag the Background layer over the New Layer button to duplicate it.

② Click Filter.

③ Click Alien Skin Snap Art.

④ Click Pen and Ink.

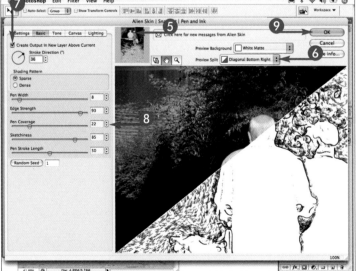

The Alien Skin Snap Art Pen and Ink dialog box appears.

⑤ Click and drag the red box over the main subject.

⑥ Click here and select a preview split.

⑦ Click here to apply the filter to a separate layer.

⑧ Click and drag any of the sliders to adjust the look.

A progress bar appears briefly, and the large preview image displays the results.

⑨ Click OK.

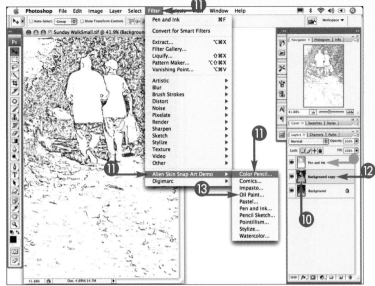

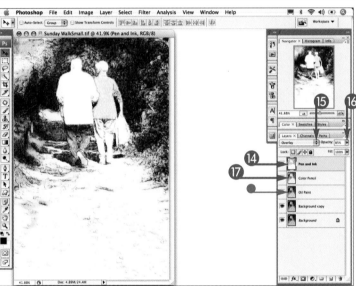

- The filter is applied to a new layer named Pen and Ink.

CHANGE THE LOOK BY ADDING OTHER FILTERS

⑩ Click the Background copy layer to select it.

⑪ Repeat steps **2** to **9** but instead select Color Pencil in step **4**.

The filter is applied to a new layer named Color Pencil.

⑫ Repeat step **10**.

⑬ Repeat steps **2** to **9** again but instead select Oil Paint in step **4**.

94

DIFFICULTY LEVEL

- The filter is applied to a new layer named Oil Paint.

⑭ Click the Pen and Ink Layer to select it.

⑮ Click here and select Overlay.

⑯ Click here and drag to slightly reduce the opacity.

⑰ Click the Color Pencil layer to select it.

⑱ Repeat steps **15** and **16**.

You can click and drag one snap art layer above or below another to change the effect.

The final image now looks like an original piece of art rather than a photograph.

TIPS

Did You Know?

Snap Art uses edge detection to outline the objects in the photo. It uses this outline to place the natural media strokes and fills areas with colors. Snap Art uses an advanced paint engine to transform your photo into an artistic composition, preserving enough detail while giving the piece a loose and artistic appearance.

Try This!

Each filter in Snap Art has many sliders and options. Move a slider to try a different look. To undo a change, press ⌘+Z (Ctrl+Z) or to redo the change, press ⌘+Y (Ctrl+Y). You can return to the default settings anytime by clicking Factory Default or pressing ⌘+R (F5) to reset the filters back to the factory defaults.

COLORIZE A BLACK-AND-WHITE
photo with AKVIS Coloriage

You can add color to a grayscale photo in Photoshop using adjustment layers, masks, and brushes; however, the Coloriage plug-in from AKVIS makes colorizing a black-and-white photograph quick and automatic. You can even use Coloriage to replace the colors in a color image. You can quickly add color to a variety of images from antique photos to hand-drawn sketches and cartoons and still maintain a very natural look.

You can colorize an image with Coloriage by clicking different colors from the Colors palette or Library and painting the colors over the areas with loose brush strokes. When you press the green forward button, the software determines the borders of the various colored areas and applies the color based on the grayscale values.

Your image must be in RGB mode. Click Image and Mode from the menu and click RGB. Then select AKVIS Coloriage from the Photoshop filters. You can select the colors from the Colors palette or use the Color Library for difficult colors such as skin, hair, and lips.

You can find Coloriage along with other AKVIS filters at http://akvis.com.

① Click and drag the background layer over the New Layer button to duplicate it.

② Click Filter.

③ Click AKVIS.

④ Click Coloriage.

The Coloriage dialog box appears, displaying your image at 100% in the Preview window.

⑤ Click here and drag to reduce or enlarge your preview.

⑥ Click here to select the first color, depending on the area.

⑦ Click here and drag to select the Pencil tool size to draw in the image.

⑧ Click and drag to draw in the image with the first color.

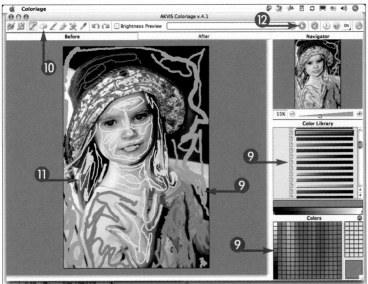

9 Repeat steps **6** to **8** to set all the colors to be used.

10 Click the Eraser tool.

11 Click and drag to correct any stray marks.

12 Click the Run button to see a preliminary colorization.

 # 95

DIFFICULTY LEVEL

● AKVIS determines the blends, and the colorized image appears in the After tab.

13 Click the Before tab and repeat steps **6** to **11** to change any colors as needed.

14 Click the Run button again to view the corrections.

15 Click the Apply button.

The final colorization is applied to the image.

Note: If the colors are too vibrant in the Background copy layer, lower the opacity of the layer slightly.

TIPS

Did You Know?
If you want to change one particular color in a color image and not alter the rest of the colors, use the Pencil tool and draw on the object. Then use the Keep-Color Pencil tool and draw a closed outline around the object.

Try This!
When you colorize a black-and-white photograph, select the less saturated colors in the Colors palette to make the colorization appear more natural. The less saturated colors are at the bottom of the palette.

More Options!
You can save the color strokes so that you can edit colors later or to vary different colorization schemes. Click the Save button after drawing all the strokes but before applying them and closing the dialog box.

Easily
SELECT THE SUBJECT AND REMOVE THE BACKGROUND
with Vertus Fluid Mask

Making selections so that you can cut out or replace backgrounds in Photoshop can be difficult and is often incomplete, especially when selecting hair or trees. You can make selections or masks more effectively with a new tool from Vertus Tech called Fluid Mask. This plug-in uses highly advanced technology that mimics the way the eye and brain look at objects.

Fluid Mask 3 automatically detects edges in the image and outlines them in blue. Depending on the

complexity of your photo, you can increase or reduce the number of objects Fluid Mask outlines by increasing or decreasing the edge sensitivity. You paint over the objects to be removed with the Delete brushes and can preview your work using the Test Render tool. Vertus Fluid Mask 3 is the most advanced tool for masking.

You can even find easy-to-follow tutorials and samples online at www.vertustech.com.

① Click and drag the Background layer over the New Layer button to duplicate it.

② Click Filter.

③ Click Vertus.

④ Click Fluid Mask.

The Fluid Mask dialog box fills the screen, and Fluid Mask automatically outlines objects in the photo.

⑤ Click here to select the Delete Local brush.

⑥ Click and drag in the image over areas to remove.

The areas turn red.

⑦ Click and drag here to adjust the brush size.

⑧ Click here to select the Delete Exact brush.

⑨ Click and drag to paint over detailed areas to be removed.

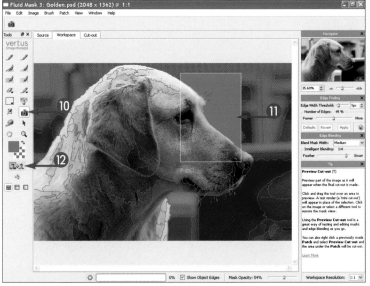

⑩ Click the Preview Cutout tool.

⑪ Click and drag over an area to preview the cutout in the selected area.

The Preview window shows the cutout subject on a green screen.

DIFFICULTY LEVEL

⑫ Click here to create the cutout.

● A progress bar appears as Fluid Mask replaces the background with the preview color in the color box.

⑬ Click File.

⑭ Click Save and Apply.

Vertus Fluid Mask removes the background and leaves the extracted foreground on a transparent layer in Photoshop.

TIPS

Did You Know?

You can click the Zoom tool and click in the image to enlarge delicate edge areas. Then paint with the Delete Exact brushes and double-click the Hand tool to return to the full view. You can also use the Blend Exact brush, the fourth brush down, to paint over areas with complex edges such as hair to further refine the selection.

More Options!

You can create an alpha mask in Photoshop from the transparency layer. Press ⌘+click (Ctrl+click) the extracted layer thumbnail in the Layers palette to select it. Click Layer → Save Selection. Give the layer a name in the dialog box and click OK. The layer is saved as a new alpha channel so that you can reselect it quickly later.

CONTROL DIGITAL NOISE
with Nik Dfine 2

Digital noise is inherent in digital photographs and appears as bright, colored specks called *chrominance noise* or dark spots or contrast noise called *luminance noise* that often look like film grain. Various factors can affect or create noise, including the light, length of exposure, and temperature when the photo is taken, as well as the peculiarities of individual cameras and sensors. You may also see more noise in photos taken using high ISO speeds and in low-light situations. Although you can reduce digital noise in a general manner with the built-in

filters in Photoshop CS3, using Nik Dfine 2 is far more powerful and enables you to control how you reduce the noise and optimize the detail. Dfine reduces luminance noise, chrominance noise, and JPG artifacts; improves contrast; and adjusts colorcasts while taking into account the effects of the noise reduction. You can reduce the noise for the whole image, for specific color ranges, or by setting control points. The large Preview screen enables you to see the improvements as you try them.

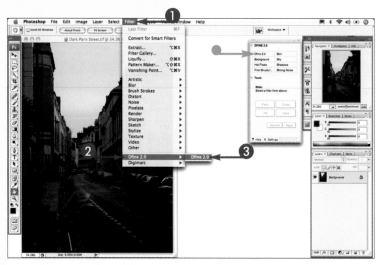

① Click Filter.

② Click Dfine 2.0.

③ Click Dfine 2.0.

● Optionally, you can click Dfine 2.0 in the Selective palette.

The Dfine dialog box appears.

④ Press ⌘+Option+0 (Ctrl+Alt+0) to view the image at 100%.

⑤ Click and drag the resize corner to get the most screen space.

⑥ Click the Pan tool.

⑦ Click and drag in the image to view an area of noise.

⑧ Click here to view a split preview vertically.

● Optionally, you can click here to view a split preview horizontally.

A red line splits the preview screen.

⑨ Click here and select Automatic.

⑩ Click Measure Noise.

DIFFICULTY LEVEL

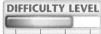

NIK Dfine 2.0 automatically measures the noise in the image, creates a profile for it, and reduces the noise in one side of the Preview image.

Note: In the figure shown here, see how much cleaner the right side appears compared to the left side.

⑪ Click OK.

The noise reduction visible in the previewed section is applied to the entire image.

TIPS

More Options!

Instead of clicking OK in step **11**, click Brush. The Dfine dialog box disappears, and a layer mask is added to the Dfine layer. Click Paint in the Dfine 2.0 palette. Click the Brush tool and paint in your image to selectively reduce noise. Use a pressure-sensitive pen tablet such as a Wacom Intuos or Cintiq for the most control with Dfine Selective.

Did You Know?

Noise reduction is more effective when applied early in the image-editing workflow. Apply Dfine 2 right after importing or converting from the Raw format. Because in-camera sharpening increases noise structures in images, you can more precisely reduce noise and preserve details with Nik Dfine 2 by turning off noise reduction and sharpening on your camera.

SHARPEN PHOTOS
with finesse using Nik Sharpener Pro 2

Sharpening is an essential step in digital imaging. Photoshop's built-in filters base the sharpening on the screen image. To get optimal image sharpening, use Sharpener Pro 2 from Nik Software. Sharpener Pro analyzes the image and sharpens according to the type of detail in the image, the type and resolution of the printer, the planned media for the print, and the intended viewing distance of the final print. You can compare the before and after images in the large preview in the dialog box prior to applying the filter. Nik Sharpener Pro 2 includes

specific sharpening settings for many of the inkjet printers on the market.

Sharpening should be the final step in the editing process to avoid introducing unwanted details in the image. Because most digital photos need some sharpening, it may be difficult to judge the quality of the image until sharpening is applied. Sharpener Pro 2 includes a Raw Presharpening filter to slightly sharpen image files at the beginning of the editing process without introducing sharpening artifacts.

① Click Filter.

② Click nik Sharpener Pro 2.0.

③ Click your output device from the list.

The nik Sharpener Pro 2.0 dialog box for the selected output device opens.

④ Click here to preview the image at a 1-to-1 ratio, or 100 percent.

⑤ Click the Viewing Distance thumbnail and select the intended viewing distance.

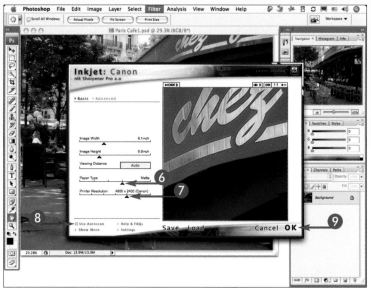

6. Click and drag the Paper Type slider to select the media.

7. Click and drag the Printer Resolution slider to match your printer's resolution.

8. Click Use Autoscan to enable Sharpener Pro to automatically adapt to the specific image.

9. Click OK.

- A progress bar appears.

  Sharpener Pro 2 applies the correct amount of sharpening according to the settings.

TIPS

Important!

The order in which you apply image enhancements affects the quality of the final print. Apply noise reduction first, if necessary. Then apply the Nik Raw Presharpening filter. Adjust the image for tone and color and resize the image. Save the image. Apply Nik Sharpener Pro 2 just prior to printing, based on the printer, media, and intended viewing distance.

More Options!

You can apply sharpening to selected areas using the Sharpener Pro 2 Selective tool. Click → Automate → nik Sharpener Pro 2.0 Selective. Click the filter in the nik Sharpener Pro 2.0 Selective palette that matches the intended output, adjust the settings, and click OK. Click Paint and click and drag in the image. Click Apply to apply the selective sharpening.

APPLY TRADITIONAL PHOTO FILTERS

such as the Sunshine filter using Nik Color Efex

Professional photographers often carry a selection of lens filters and light reflectors to take advantage of every lighting condition they might encounter. You can achieve similar effects using Color Efex Pro 2 from Nik Software. Nik filters can help you enhance images better than using Photoshop alone. Based on photographic filter technology, these filters consider the existing color and light in an image and adapt the effect accordingly. The filters can adapt to any previous adjustments in the photo, so you can apply multiple filters in a different order and achieve more

natural-looking photographic enhancements. You can use any of the Color Efex Pro filters and customize the settings to control the light and color in your digital images. You can even save your settings to apply them to a range of photos for a consistent workflow and increased productivity.

The Sunshine filter shown in this task is just one of the many traditional styled filters. It transforms the grayed colors from a photo shot on an overcast day into a bright colorful scene, yet in a very natural way.

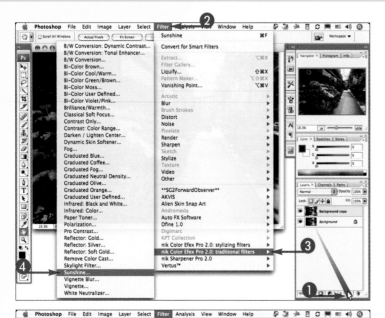

1 Click and drag the Background layer over the New Layer button.

2 Click Filter.

3 Click nik Color Efex Pro 2.0: traditional filters.

4 Click Sunshine.

The Sunshine filter dialog box appears.

5 Click here to select a split preview.

6 Click the + signs to enlarge the preview images.

7 Click and drag the Saturation Correction slider to control the intensity of the colors.

8 Click and drag the Cool Color Reduction slider to manipulate the blue colors.

9 Click the Light Casting Algorithm thumbnail and select the type of sunlight to add.

10 Click and drag the Light Intensity slider to control the amount of added light.

11 Click and drag the Radius slider to control the increased detail smoothing.

12 Click the Select Prefilter thumbnail and select a color contrast filter to enhance different colors and objects.

13 Click and drag the Prefilter Strength slider to change the amount of the prefilter added to the image.

14 Click OK.

#99

DIFFICULTY LEVEL

● A progress bar appears as Color Efex Pro applies the filter to the image.

15 Click the Visibility icon for the Background copy layer on and off to compare the results with the original.

TIPS

Did You Know?

Nik Color Efex Pro 2 includes traditional Reflector filters, Infrared conversions, and Cross Processing filters, as well as a Selective tool with the filters on a separate floating palette. Use the Selective palette to apply any of the filters with a paintbrush to control the location and amount of the effect. Use a Wacom pen tablet for even greater control.

Try This!

If Photoshop does not display all of your third-party plug-ins, install them into a separate folder that you create and name inside the Photoshop application folder or even elsewhere on your hard drive. Launch Photoshop, click Photoshop (Edit) → Preferences → Plug-Ins & Scratch Disks. Click Additional Plug-ins Folder. Click Choose and navigate to select your additional plug-ins folder.

TRAVEL BEYOND THE BRIDGE
with Extensis Portfolio 8

Extensis Portfolio 8 is a unique tool for organizing and managing all kinds of digital files. Portfolio enables you to share files in a variety of ways, from CDs or DVDs to searchable Web sites. You can quickly find a specific file whether it is stored on your computer or on any external drive, CD, or DVD. Because of its added functionality, Portfolio goes beyond the capabilities of the Photoshop CS3 Bridge or any other software for managing digital assets. Portfolio is the most flexible way to catalog, archive, track, share, and locate your files. Use Portfolio to

download your photos to your computer, rename the files, and include any Exif, XMP, or catalog data you want. Portfolio adds thumbnails and screen previews to the database. You can burn a CD or DVD of the original images to create an archival copy from within Portfolio's catalog dialog box. By including the read-only browser on the CD or DVD, you can quickly search those files even from another computer. Portfolio's powerful database tracks your files and gives you a visual preview of any image wherever it is stored.

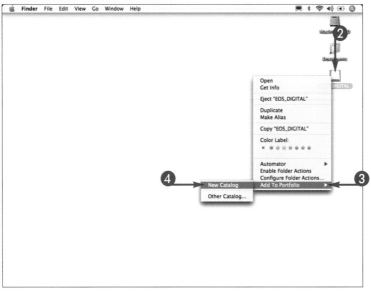

CREATE A CATALOG OF IMAGES

1. Insert a digital media card into your card reader.

2. Press Control+click (right-click) the digital media icon on the desktop.

3. Click Add To Portfolio.

4. Click New Catalog.

Portfolio opens a Save dialog box for the new catalog.

5. Type a name for the catalog.

6. Click here and select the location to save your catalog.

7. Click Save.

The Use Screen Preview dialog box appears with Enable Screen Previews selected by default.

8. Click Done to enable the previews.

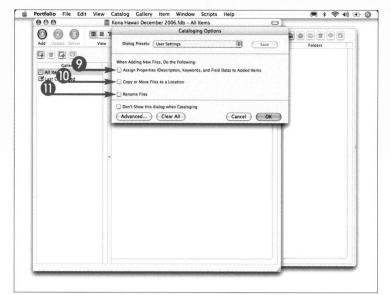

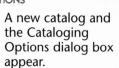

100

DIFFICULTY LEVEL

A new catalog and the Cataloging Options dialog box appear.

9 Click Assign Properties.

The Cataloging Options dialog box expands.

10 Click Copy or Move Files to a Location.

The dialog box expands again.

11 Click Rename Files.

The dialog box expands again.

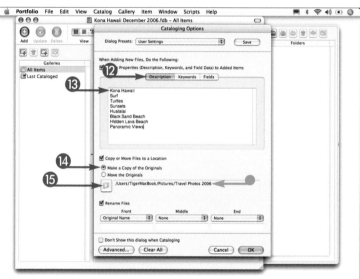

12 Click the Description tab.

13 Type data in the left field for your images.

14 Click Make a Copy of the Originals.

15 Click the Folder icon.

16 Navigate to the location for the catalog in the dialog box that appears and click Choose.

● The location appears in the field.

TIPS

Try This!

Burn a CD of the original images. From the menu, click Gallery and Burn to Disc. Click Original Files and Link Paths in Catalog to Files Burned to Disc. Type a folder name. Click Create a Catalog and type the catalog name. Click the other empty check boxes to include the Portfolio Browser applications on the CD and click Burn.

More Options!

You can rotate JPEG images from portrait to landscape orientation or vice versa from within Portfolio without having to launch another program. Click an image or press ⌘+click (Ctrl+click) any number of JPEG images to select them. Then press Control+click (right-click) to open the menu. Select the type of rotation to use. Portfolio rotates the image for you.

TRAVEL BEYOND THE BRIDGE
with Extensis Portfolio 8

Portfolio can catalog almost any type of digital file. You can add individual files, folders, or complete volumes such as a CD or a hard drive by simply dragging the file, folder, or disk icon into an open catalog window. However, using the Instant Cataloging feature described in this task offers more options and control over the way Portfolio stores the information. By entering descriptions, keywords, or information in the custom fields, you can organize your files more easily. You can then customize

Portfolio to display images in galleries and to view images as thumbnails, lists, or individual items with all the stored data. To find a particular file, you can search with Portfolio's Quick Find, located on the toolbox, using any words or phrase you entered when cataloging the file. You can also search using the Find command and search for specific criteria associated with the file.

Portfolio offers many more advantages that you can find on the www.extensis.com Web site.

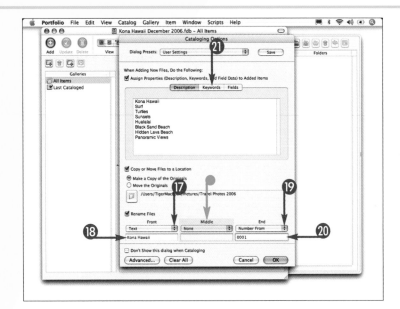

⑰ Click here and select Text.

⑱ Type a name in the data field.

● Optionally, you can repeat steps **17** and **18** to set the middle part of the filenames.

⑲ Click here and select Number From.

⑳ Type a starting number for the images in this catalog.

㉑ Click the Keywords tab.

The dialog box changes options.

㉒ Type a keyword here.

㉓ Click the + to add the keyword to the list below.

● Optionally, you can click the Fields tab and select the data to edit.

㉔ Click OK.

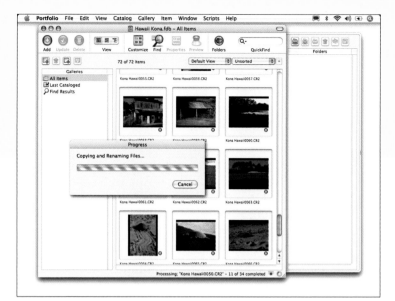

A progress bar appears.

Note: *The time required to copy, catalog, and rename your files depends on the number and size of the files, as well as the speed and type of connection of the card reader.*

Portfolio displays a partial catalog as it completes the process.

VIEW AN IMAGE AND ITS PROPERTIES

㉕ Click the image thumbnail.

㉖ Click the Preview button.

Portfolio displays a larger preview of the photo.

㉗ Click the Properties button to view details of the image data.

CUSTOMIZE THE CATALOG

㉘ Click the Customize button to make changes or make different data appear in the catalog.

TIP

Did You Know?

Portfolio 8 includes a separate application called Portfolio Express that enables you to find cataloged files without launching the complete application. After you launch Portfolio Express, you can keep it running in the background and hide or show the palette using a hot key. The compact Portfolio Express palette floats above other document windows. Use the QuickFind feature from the palette to find a particular image and double-click a thumbnail in the Portfolio Express palette to edit the original image. You can also drag and drop the thumbnail onto an alias (shortcut) of Photoshop to open it. You can even drag a thumbnail directly into an email message to send a copy of the original file as an attachment.

Index

Numbers

32-bit High Dynamic Range (HDR) images, 124–125

A

B

Index

Index

Index

Index

Index